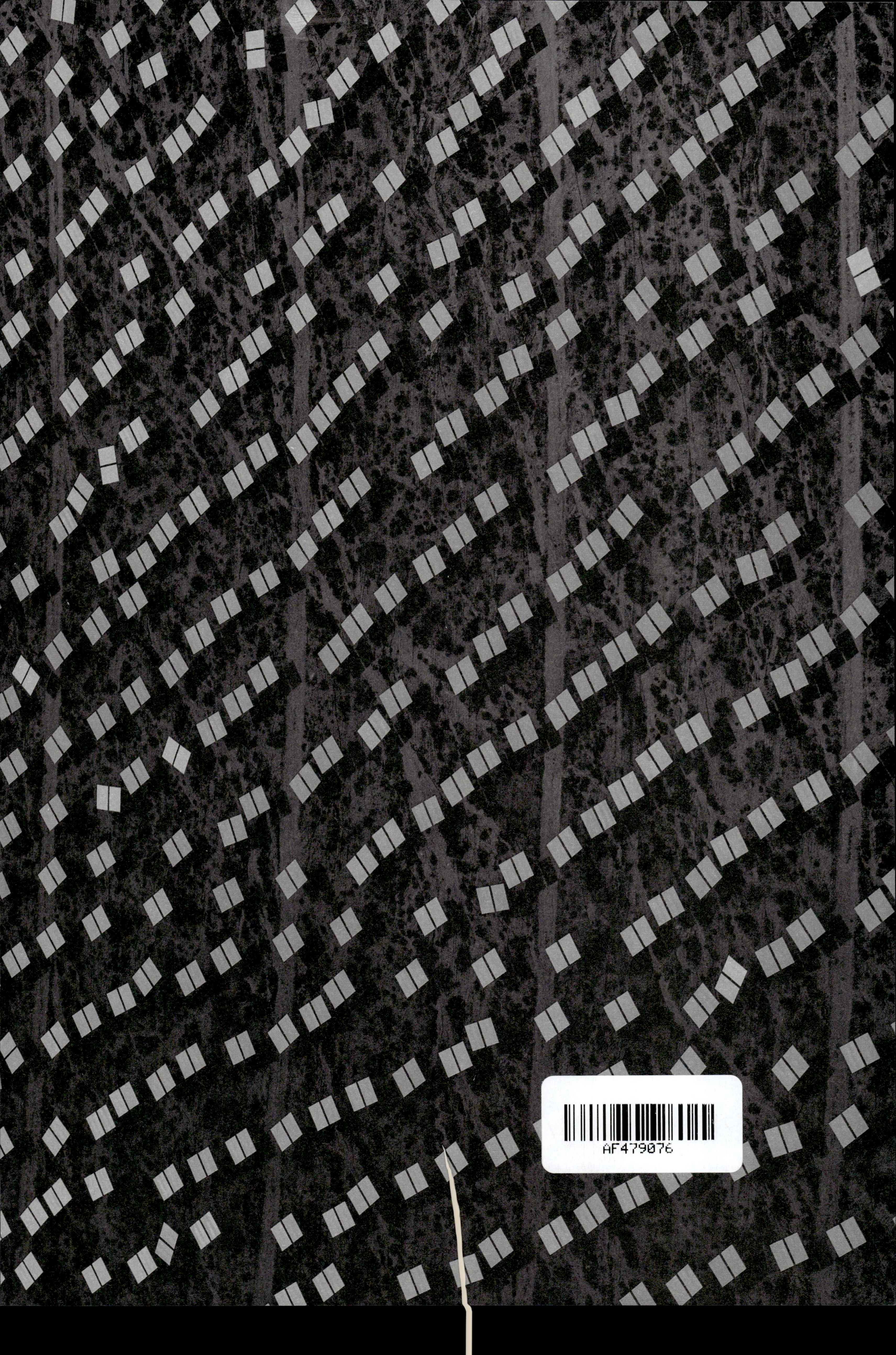

CONTENTS

PLATES

#26, 15 OCTOBER 2010

SITE OF IVANPAH SOLAR ELECTRIC GENERATING SYSTEM (IVANPAH) PRIOR TO COMMENCEMENT OF CONSTRUCTION, MOJAVE DESERT, CALIFORNIA, USA

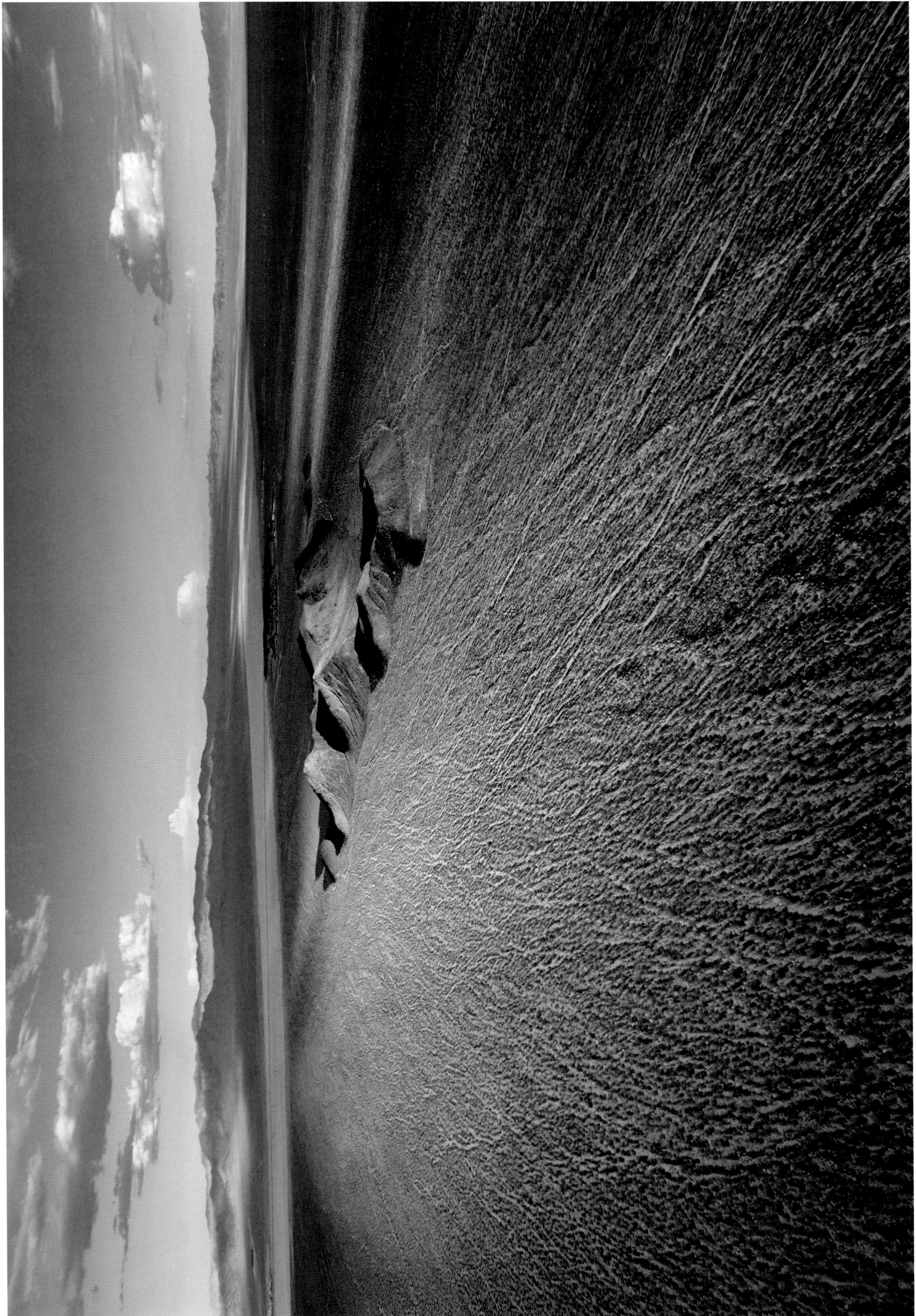

#5490, 6 JANUARY 2012

NATURAL EROSION GULLIES OF ALLUVIAL SLOPE OVERLAP WITH BOUNDARY AND SERVICE ROADS OF UNIT 2

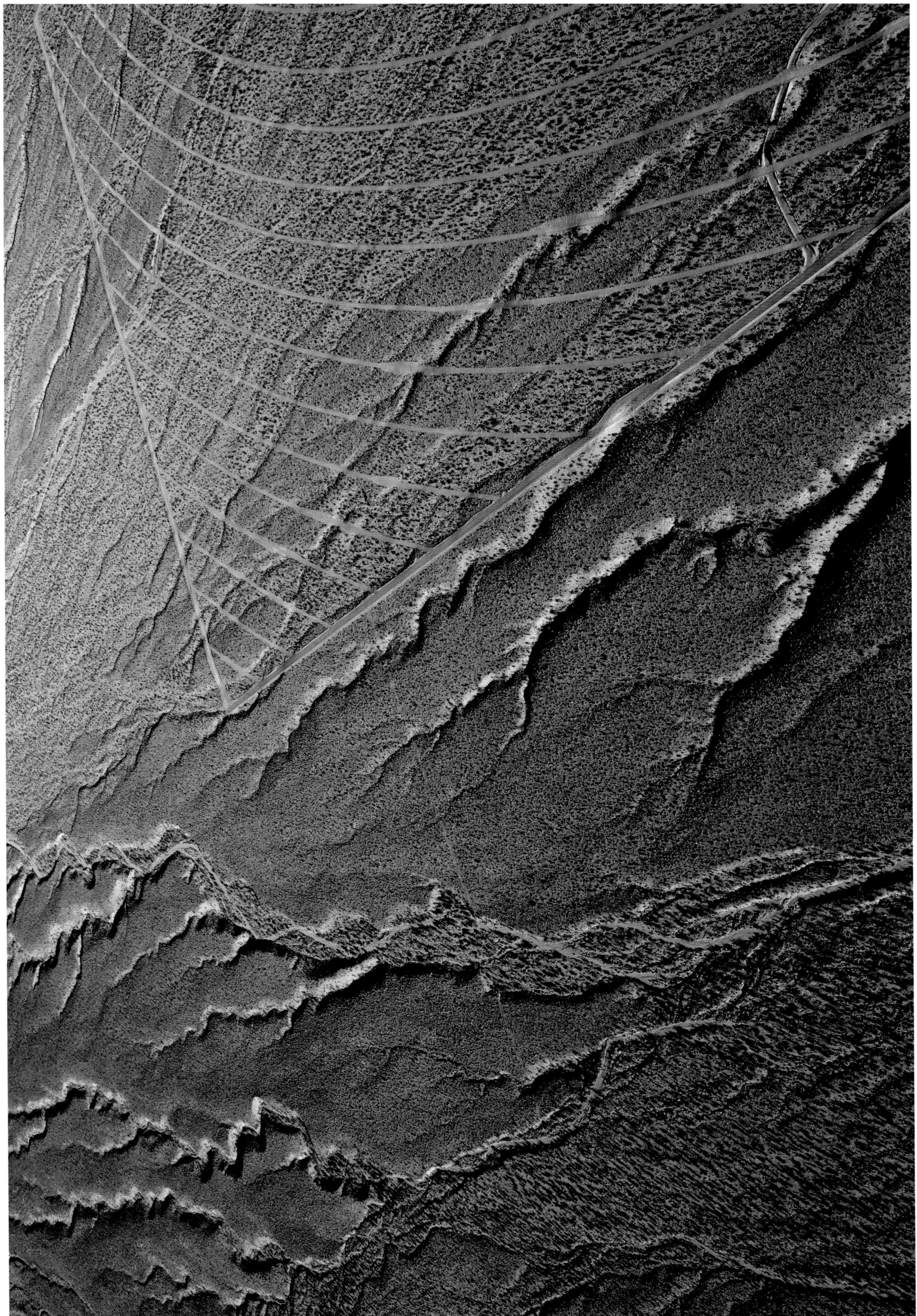

#6536, 2 JUNE 2012

DETAIL OF CONCENTRIC SERVICE ROADS IN UNIT 3 PRIOR TO PYLON AND HELIOSTAT INSTALLATION

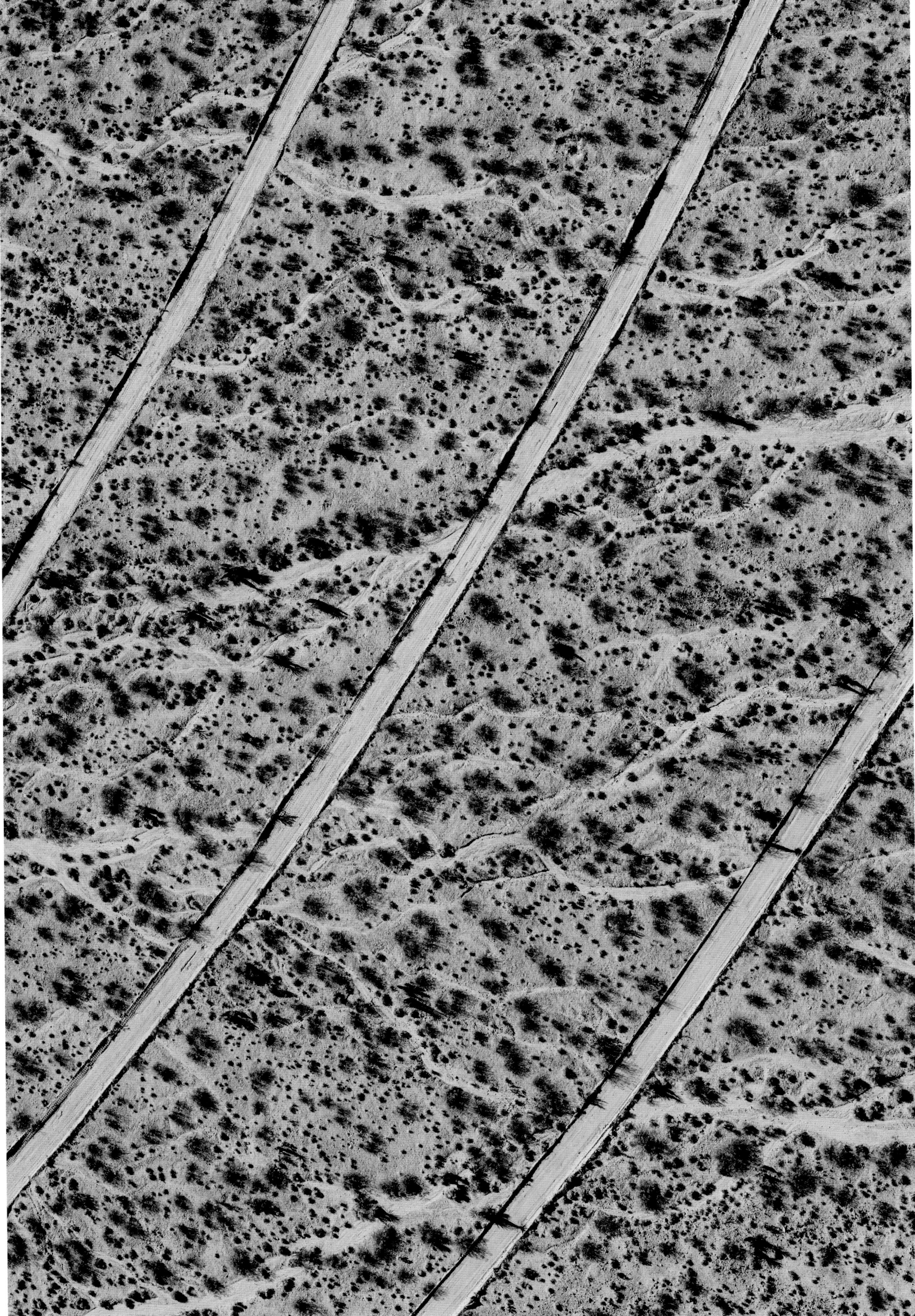

#584, 14 JANUARY 2011

INITIAL EXCAVATION FOR FUTURE SUBSTATION, OPERATIONS CENTER, AND CONSTRUCTION BLOCK WITH CLARK MOUNTAIN IN THE BACKGROUND

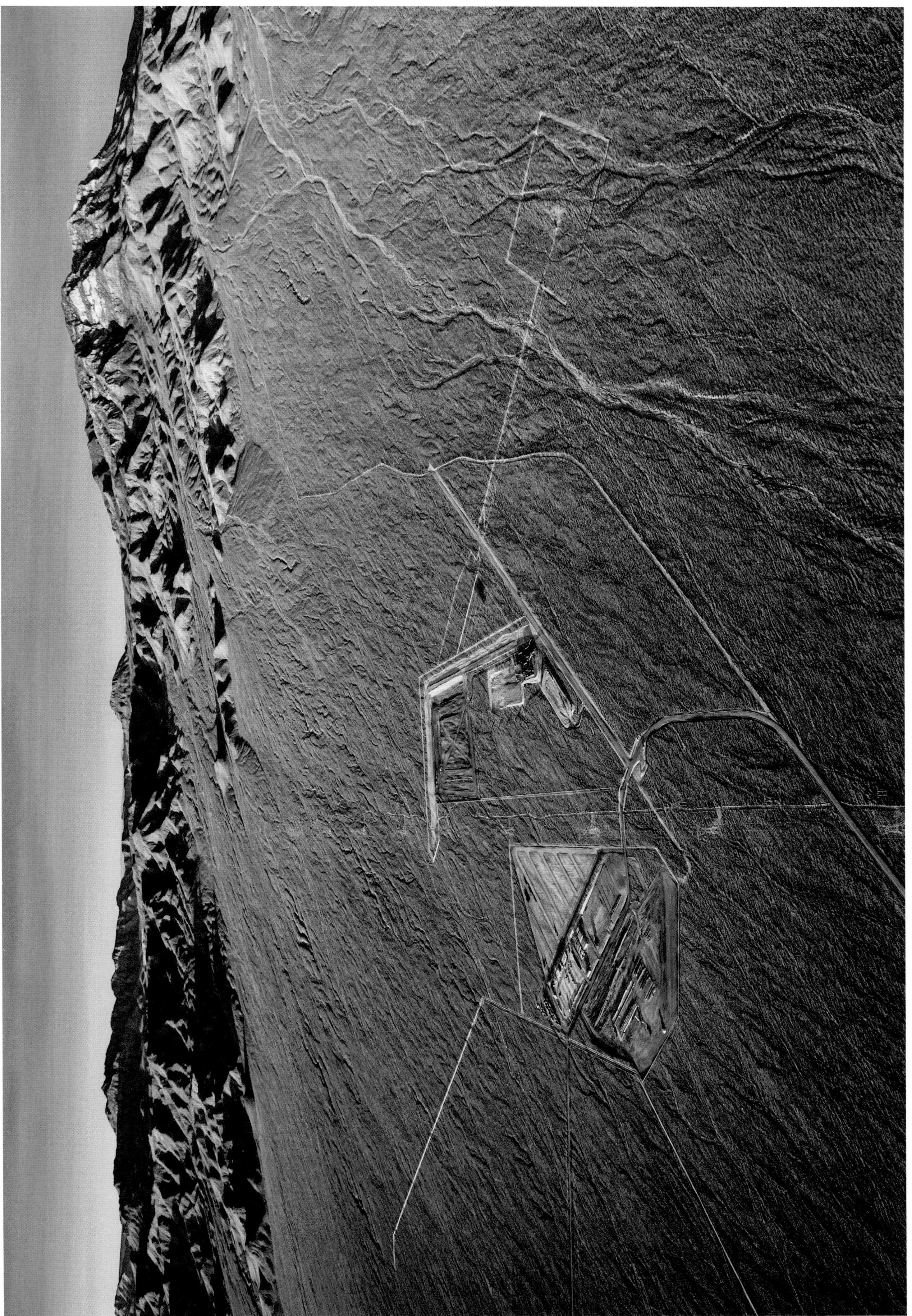

#897, 14 JANUARY 2011

DETAIL OF INITIAL EXCAVATION AND GROUND PREPARATION NEAR EXISTING GRID TRANSMISSION LINES

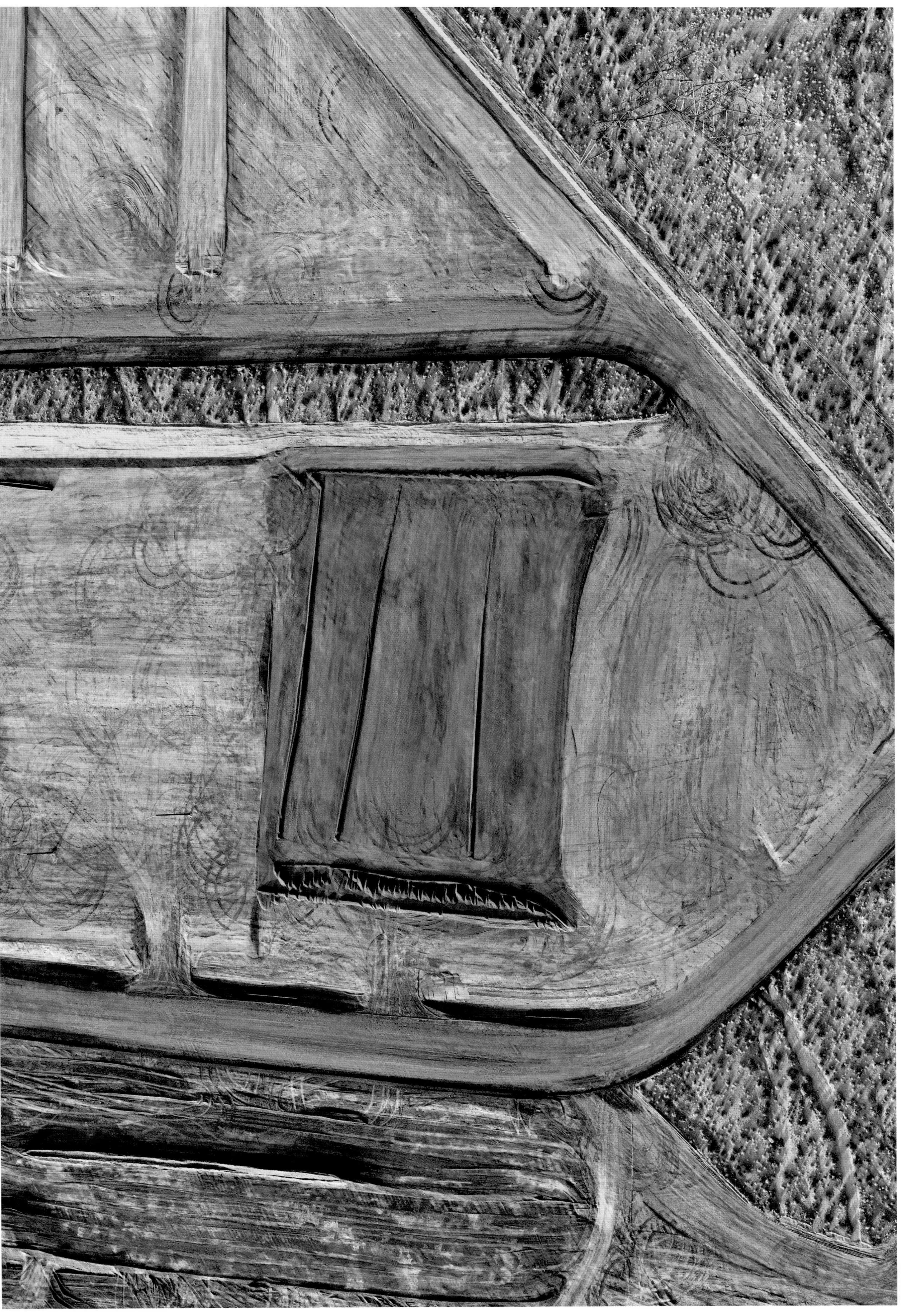

#680, 14 JANUARY 2011

EARLY EXCAVATION AND EARTH MOVING FOR UNIT 1 POWER BLOCK

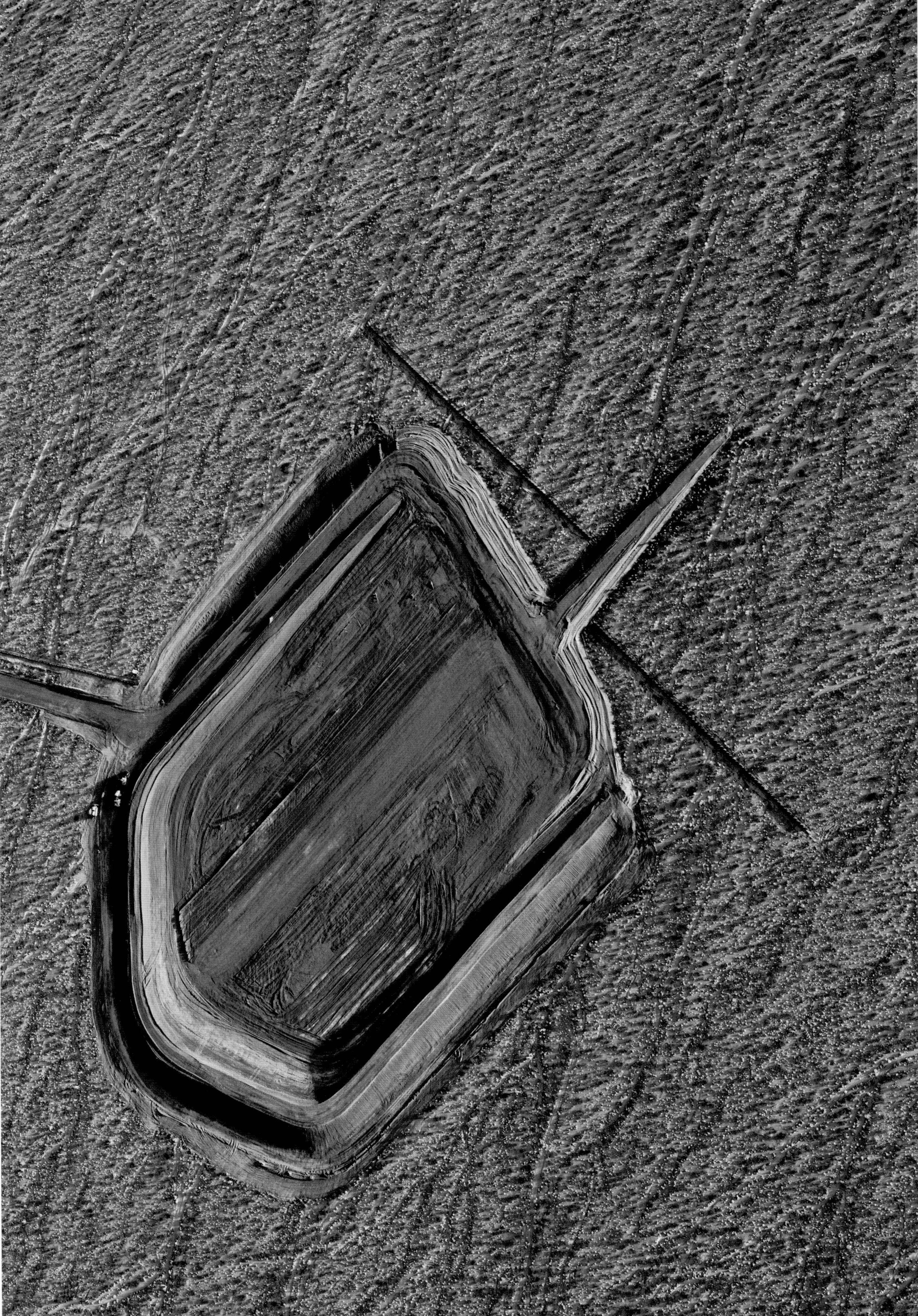

#3995, 28 JULY 2011

DETAIL OF UNIT 2 POWER BLOCK EXCAVATION AND PREPARATION

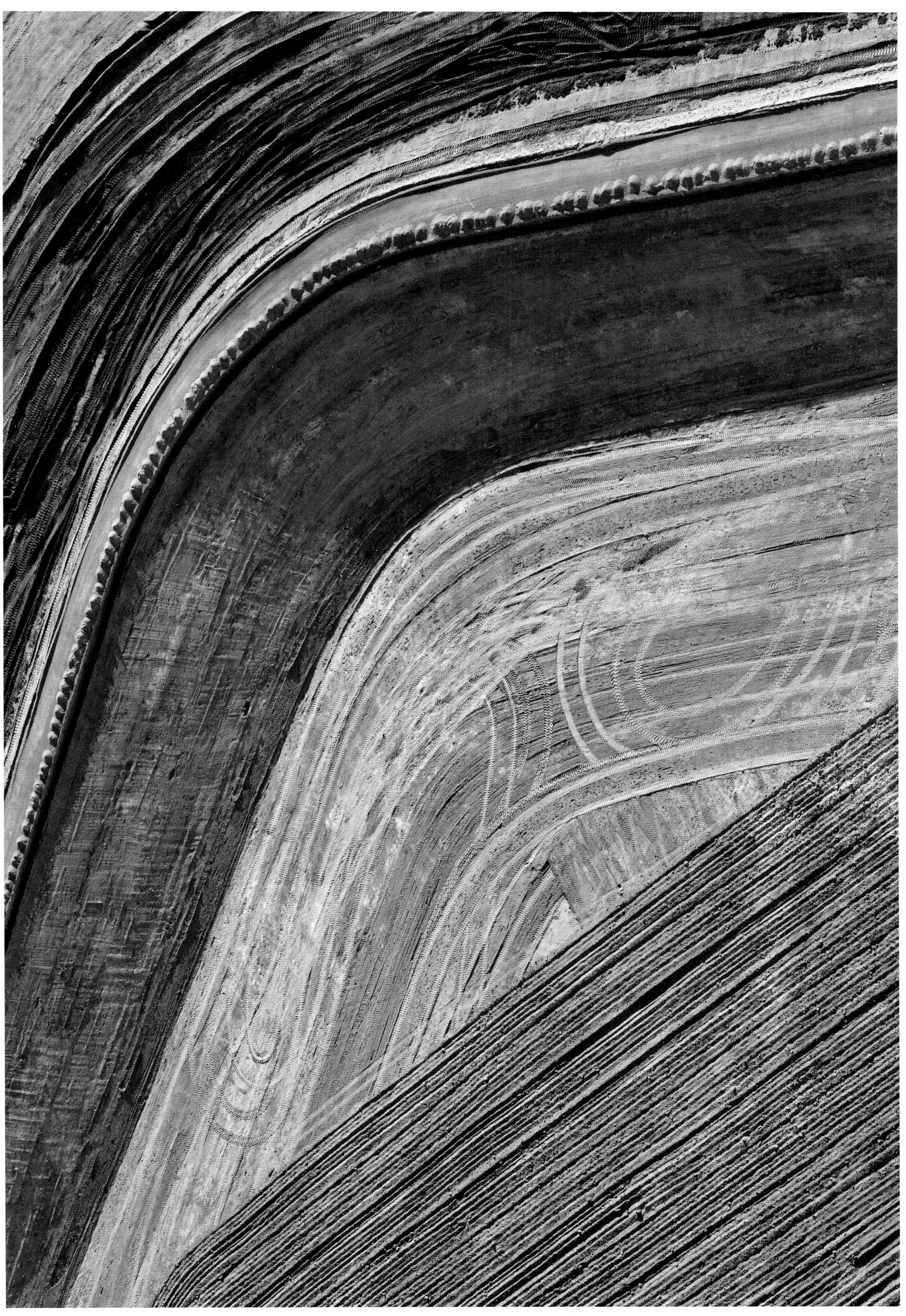

#4023, 28 JULY 2011

UNIT 3 POWER BLOCK CONSTRUCTION WITH VIEW TOWARD PRIMM, NEVADA

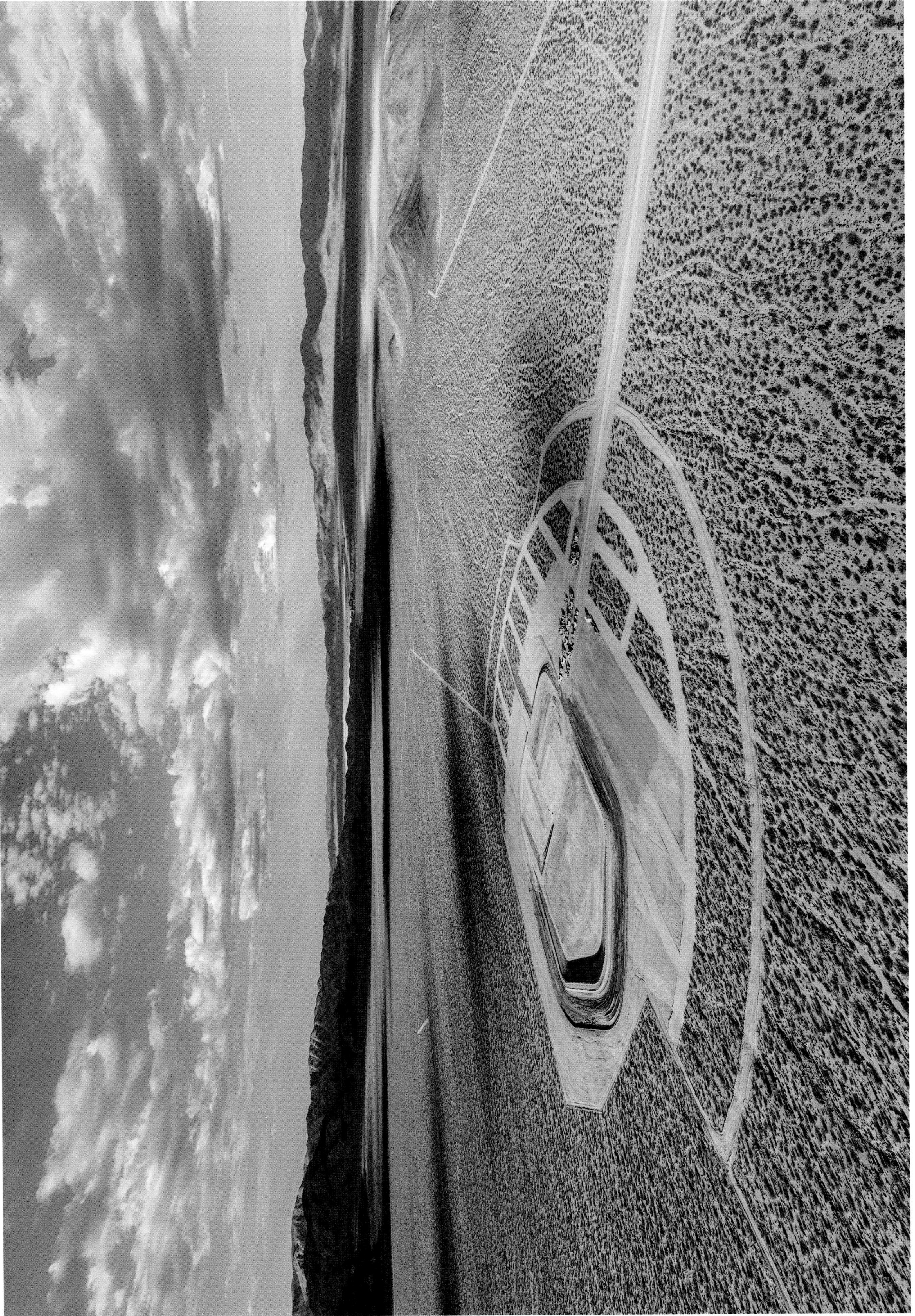

#702, 14 JANUARY 2011

EARLY EXCAVATION FOR SUBSTATION, OPERATIONS CENTER, AND CONSTRUCTION BLOCK

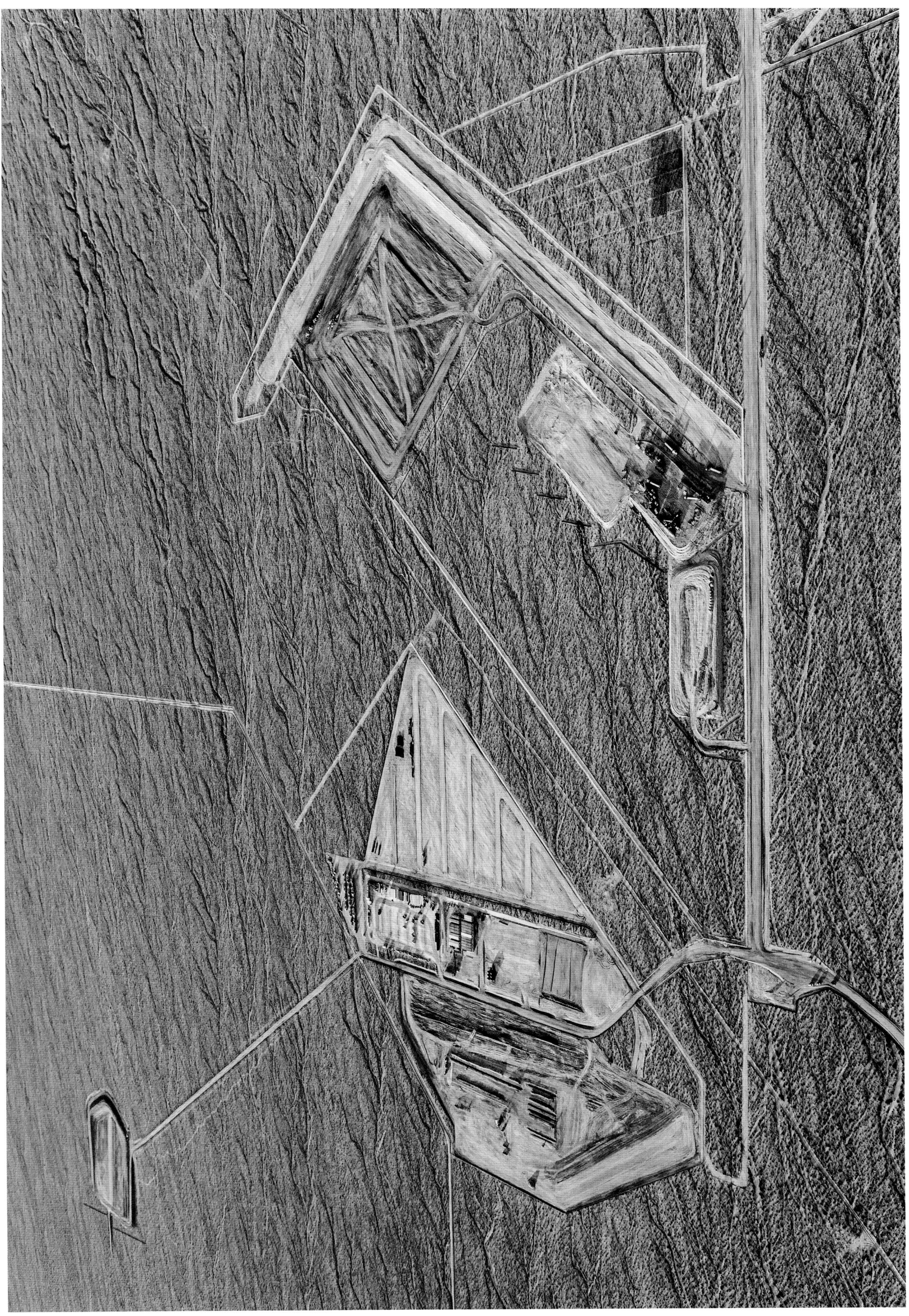

#5584, 6 JANUARY 2012

EARTH EXCAVATION AND GROUND PREPARATION OF UNIT 2

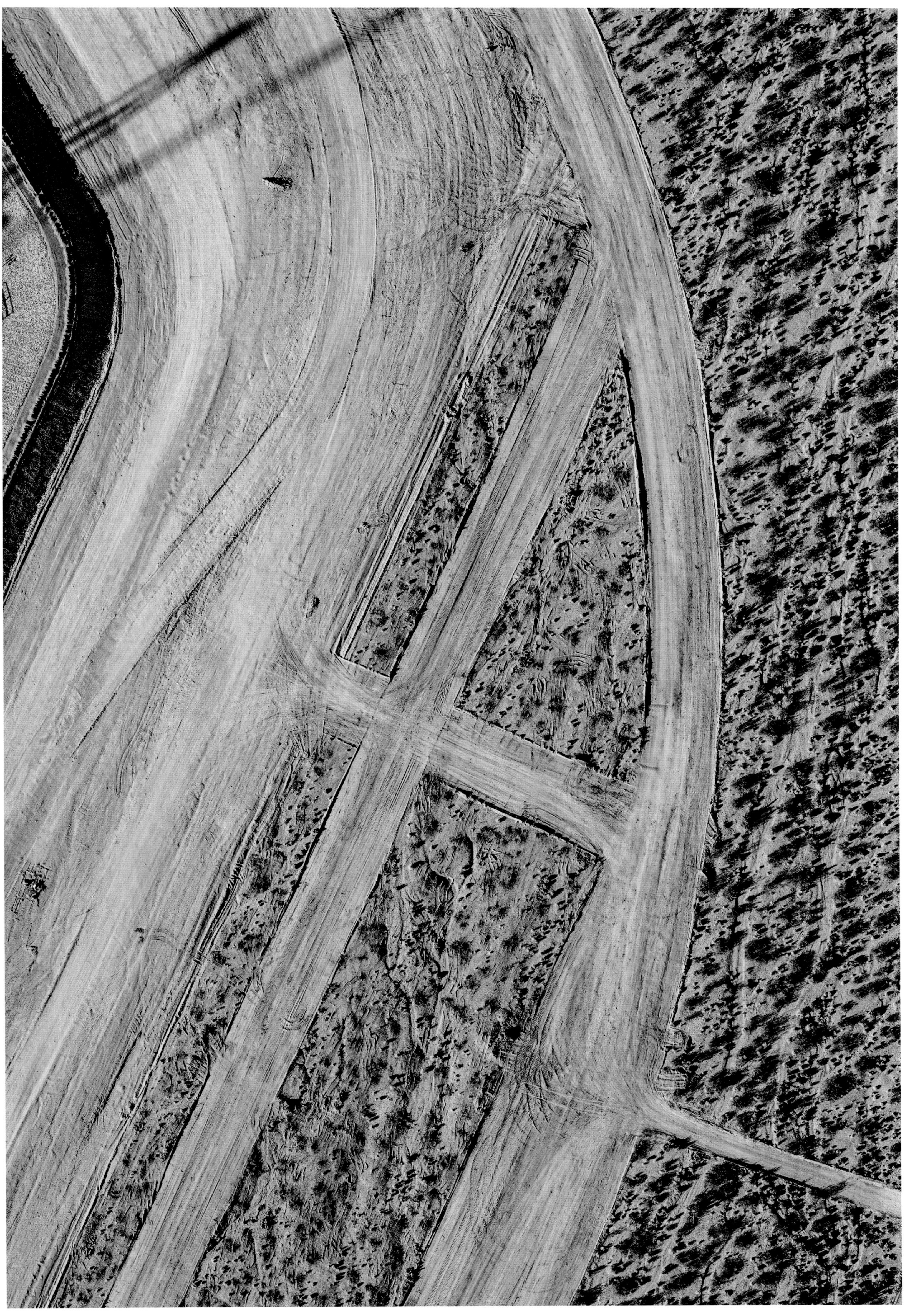

#4061, 28 JULY 2011

EXCAVATION WORK FOR UNIT 3 POWER BLOCK

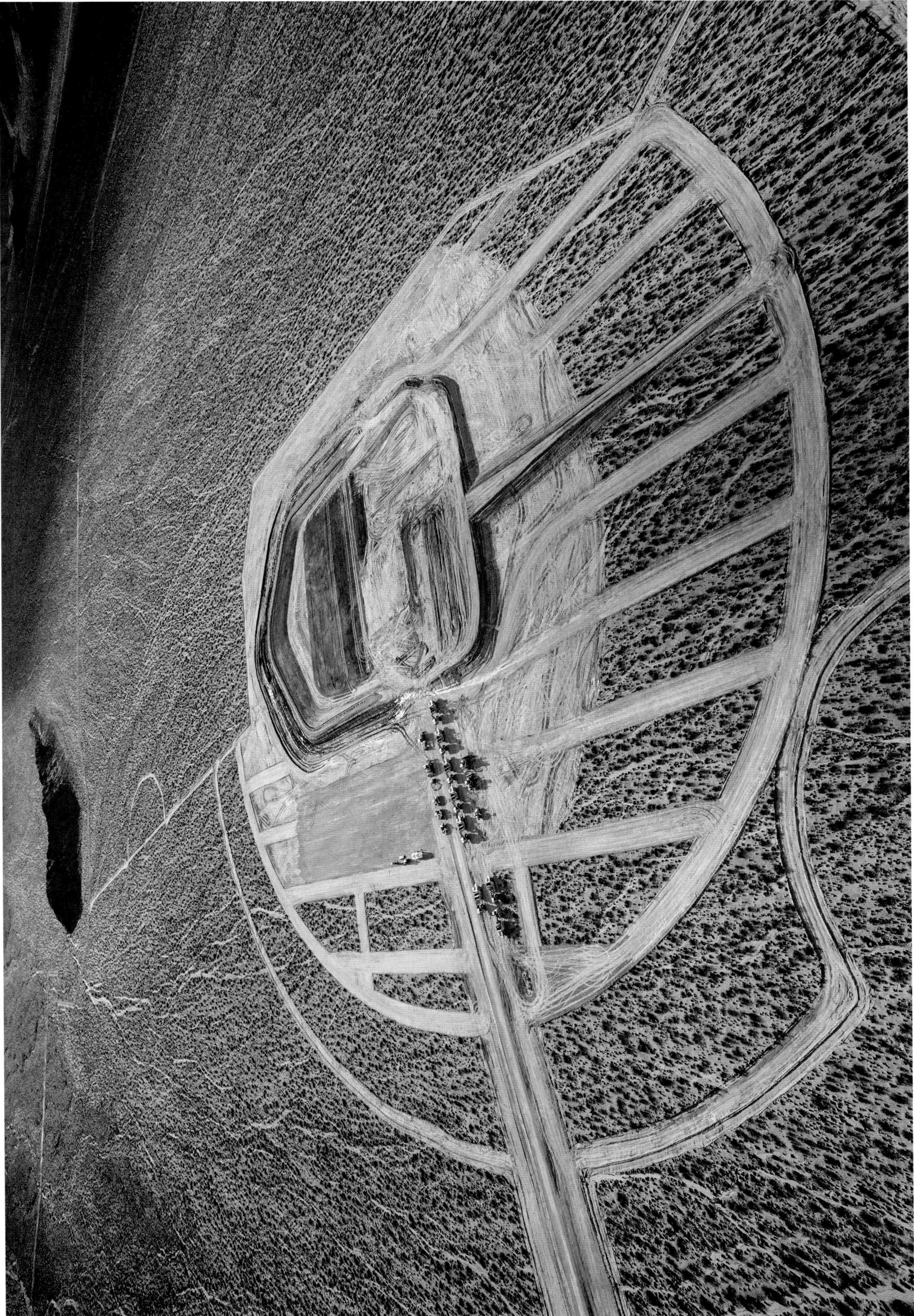

#3966, 28 JULY 2011

EARTH MOVING EQUIPMENT FOR UNIT 2

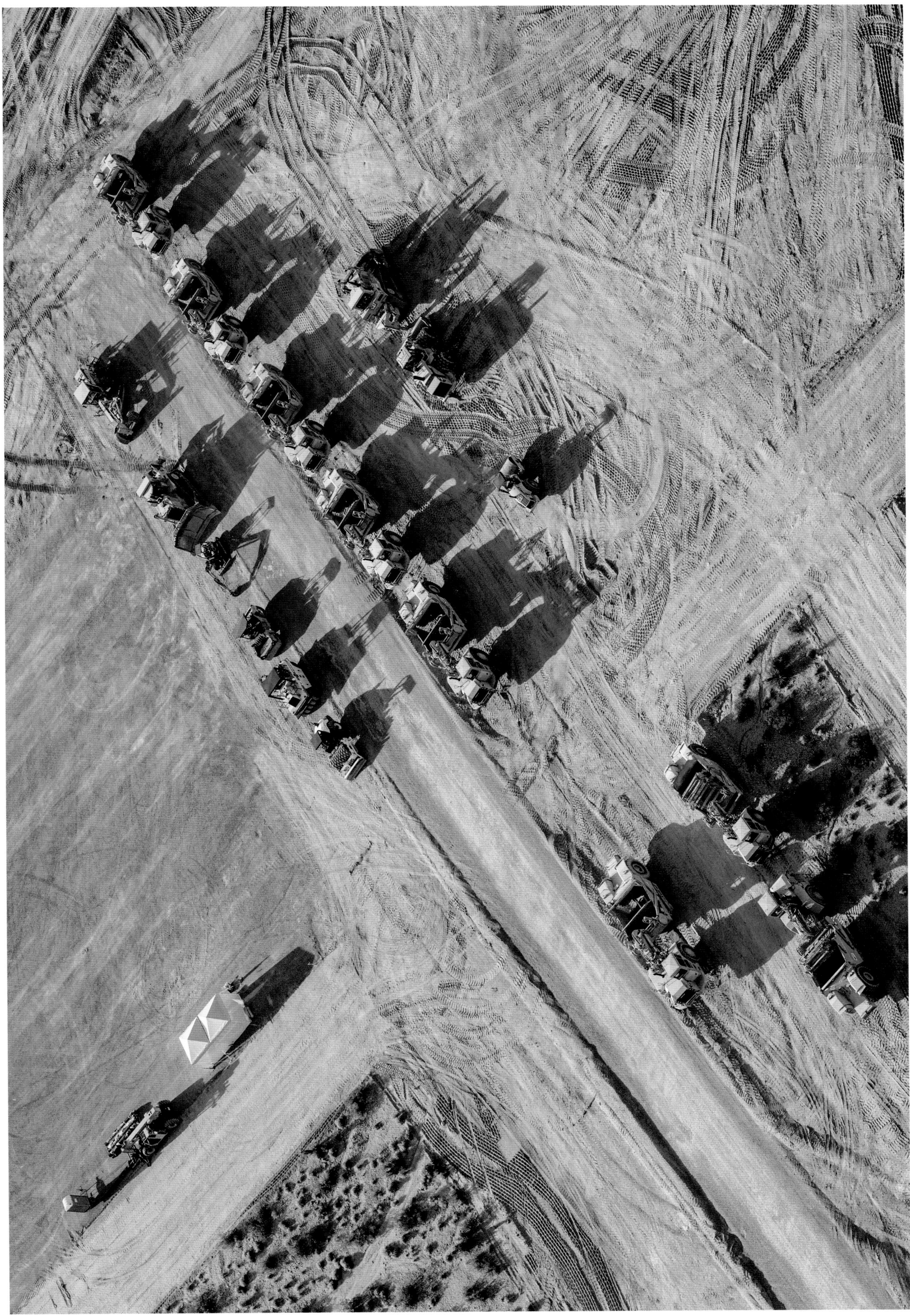

#1157, 21 APRIL 2011

EXCAVATION AND GROUND PREPARATION FOR FUTURE SUBSTATION

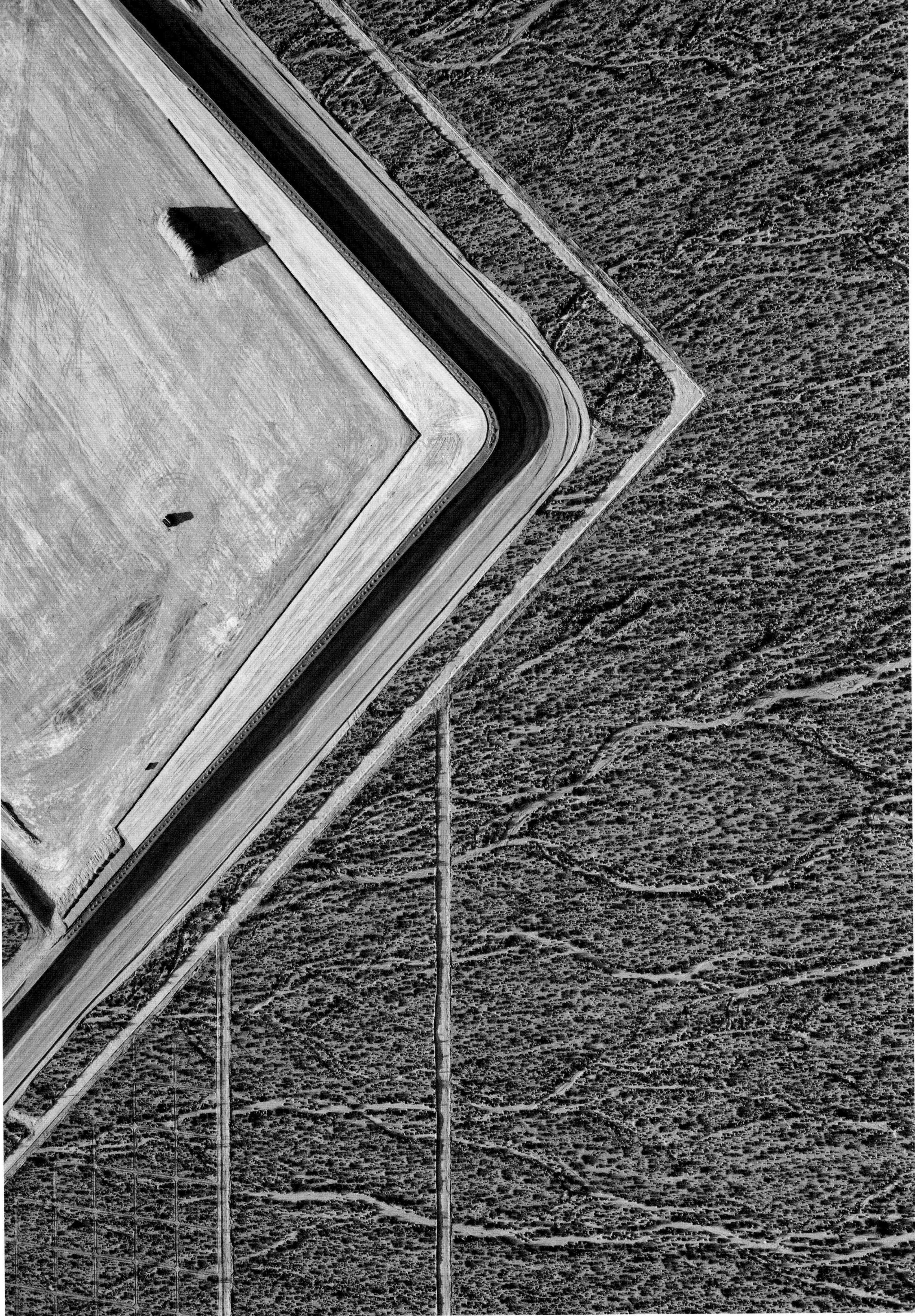

#1515, 21 APRIL 2011

CONSTRUCTION BLOCK AT UNIT 1

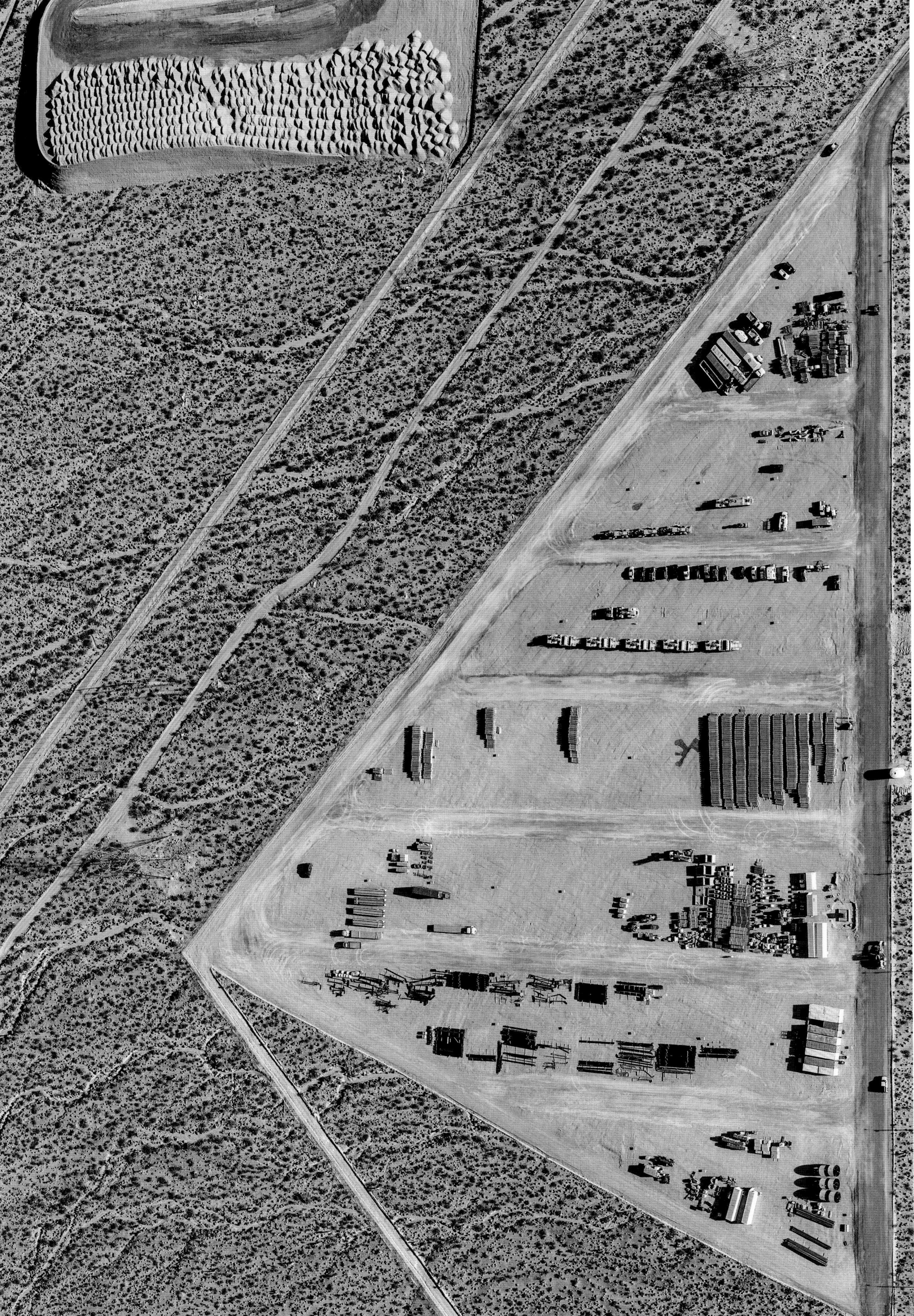

#4461, 28 JULY 2011

CONCRETE FOUNDATION POUR FOR UNIT 2

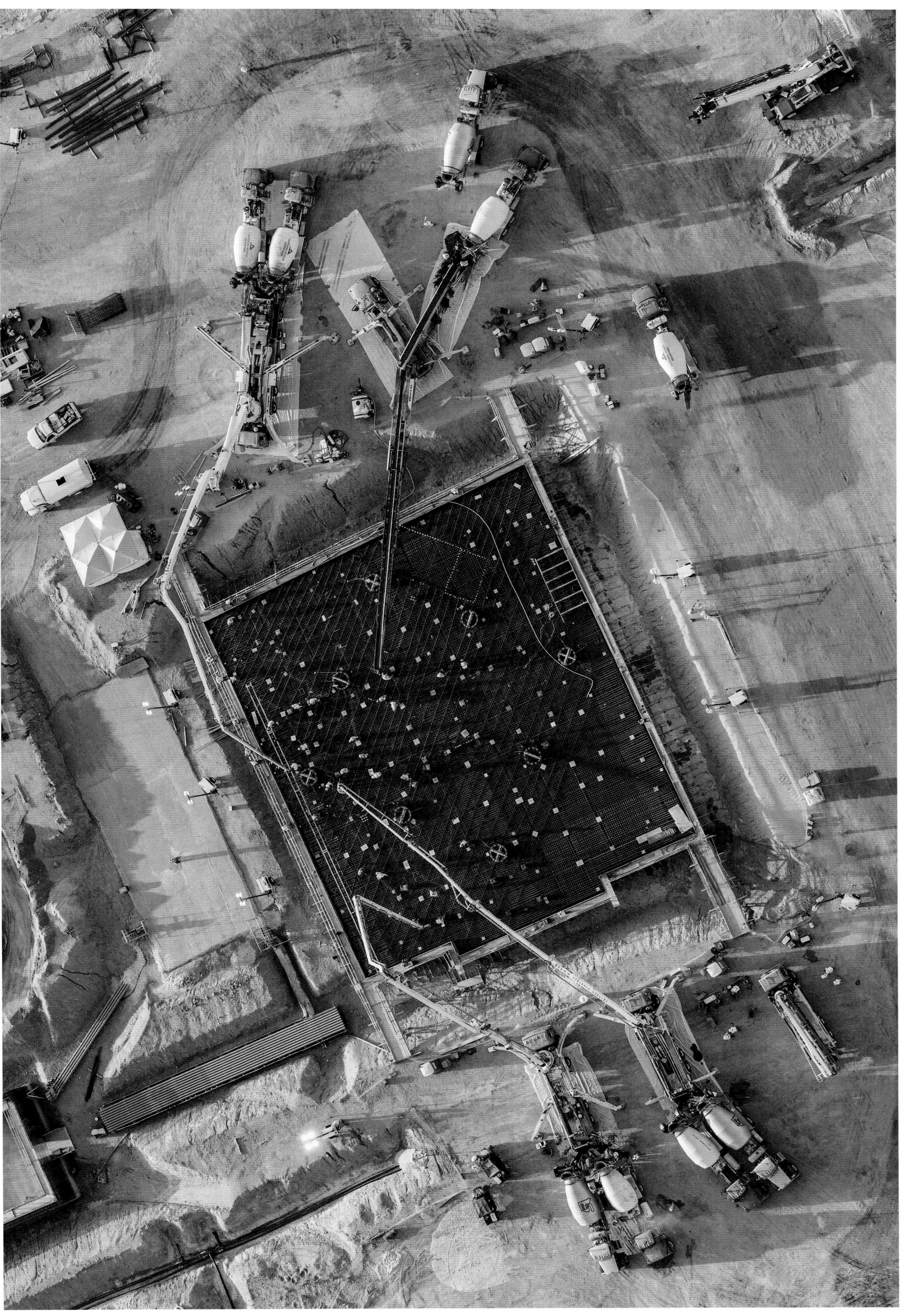

#1548, 21 APRIL 2011

CONCENTRIC CIRCLES OF SERVICE ROADS AROUND CONSTRUCTION OF UNIT 1 POWER BLOCK

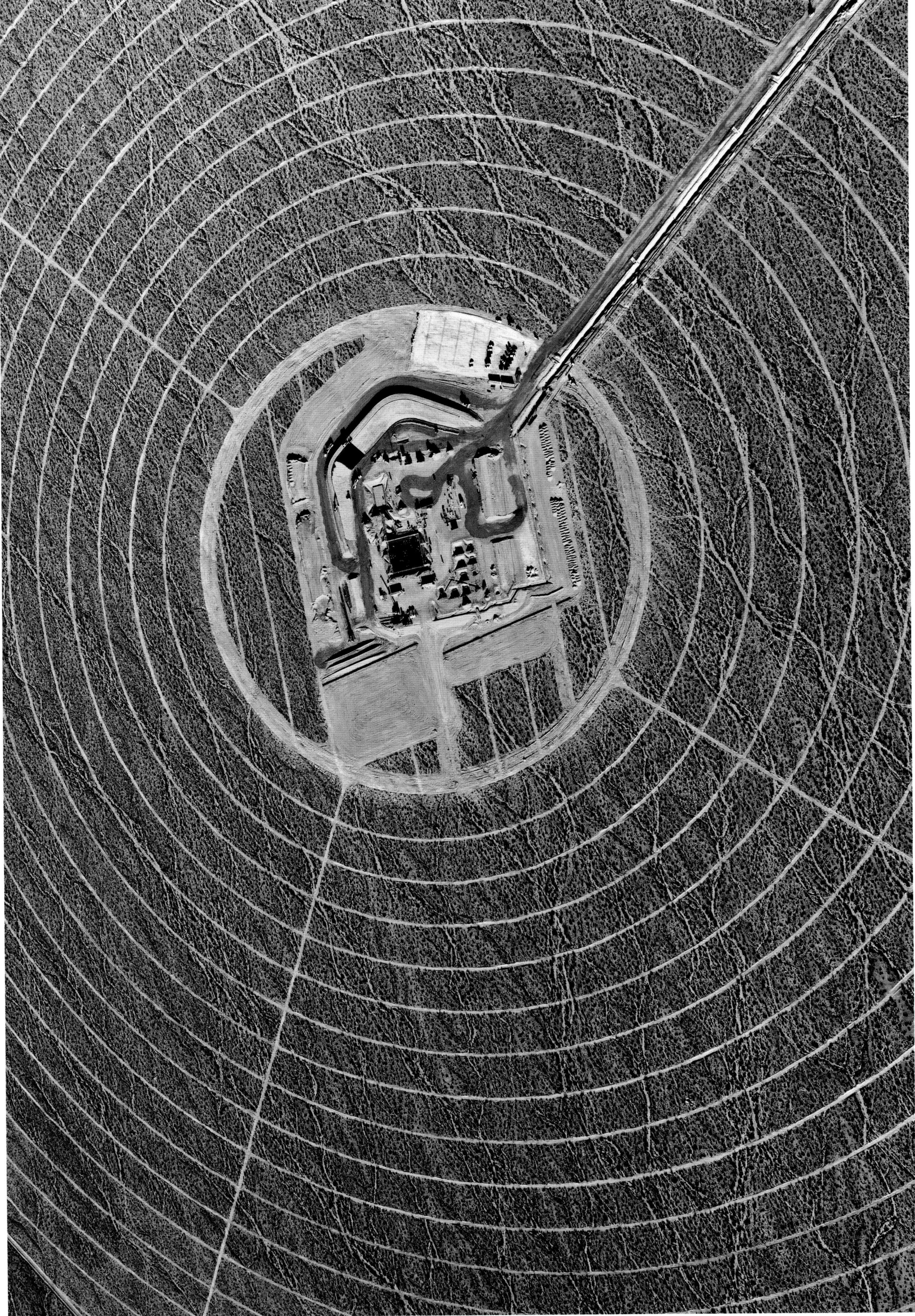

#7031, 2 JUNE 2012

UNITS 2 AND 3 SKIRT THE BASE OF A HILL RISING ABOVE ALLUVIAL SLOPE WITH PRIMM, NEVADA, TO THE NORTH

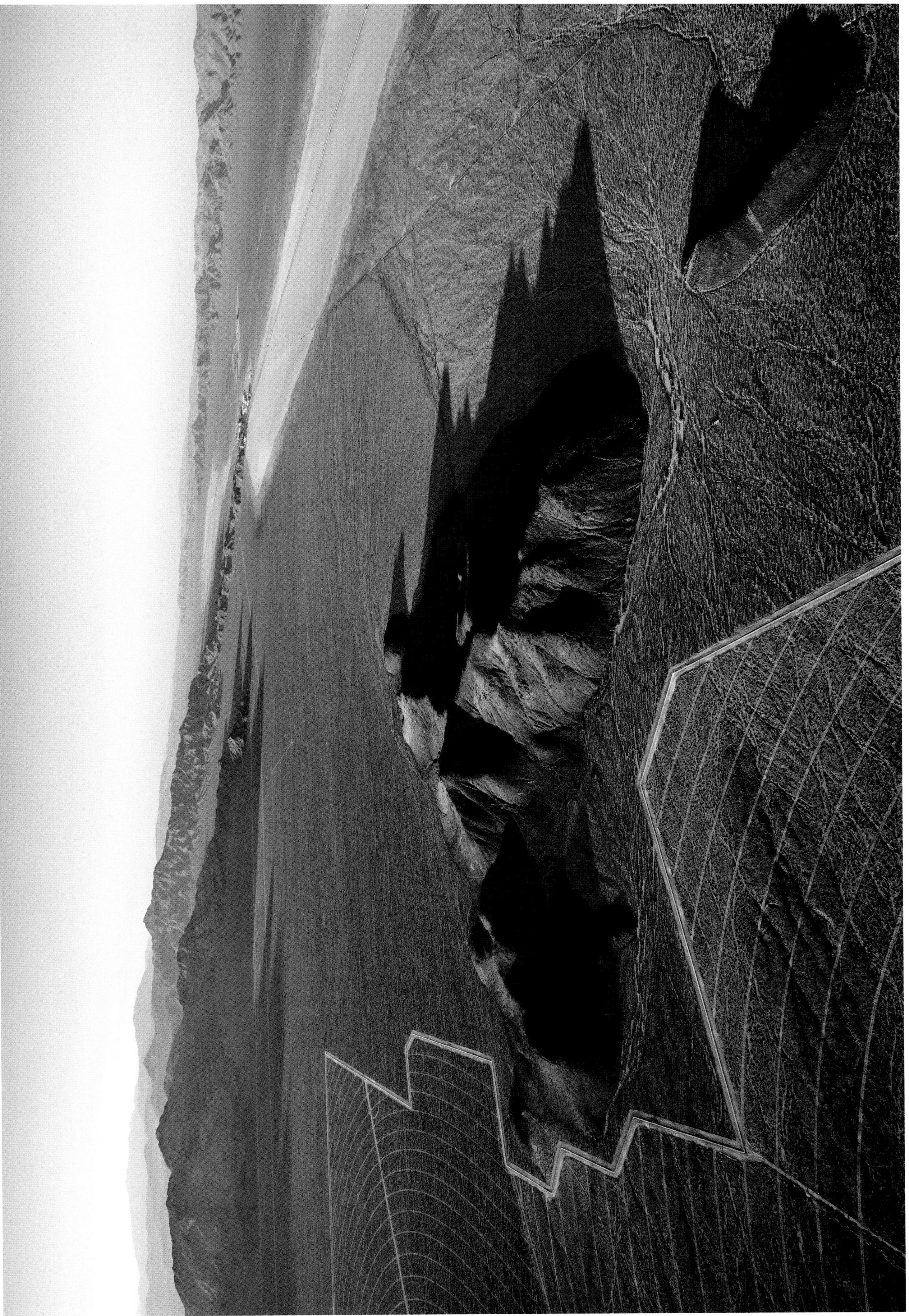

#5451, 6 JANUARY 2012

NATURAL EROSION GULLIES OF ALLUVIAL SLOPE OVERLAP WITH BOUNDARY AND SERVICE ROADS OF UNIT 2

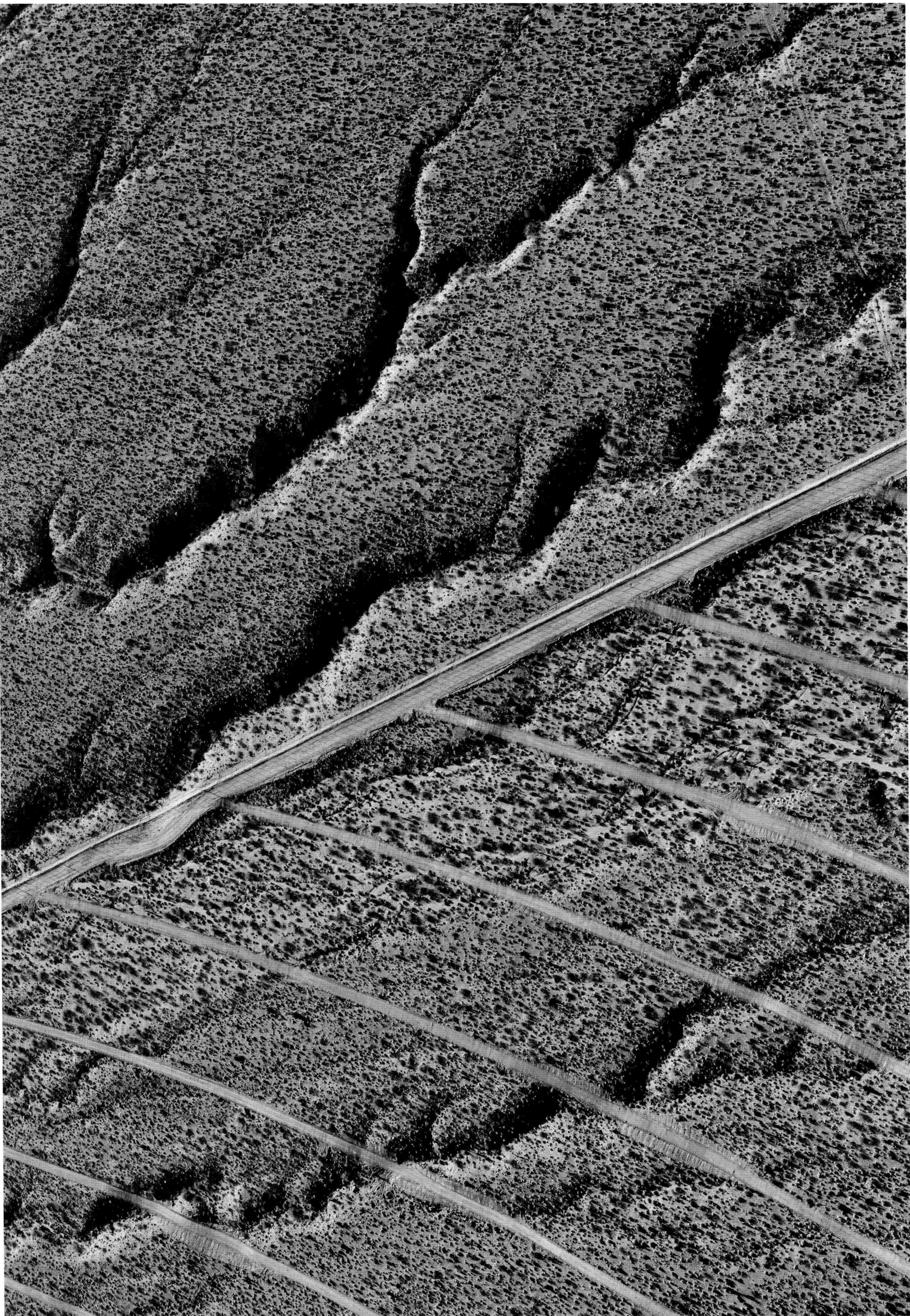

#1574, 21 APRIL 2011

POWER BLOCK CONSTRUCTION AND SERVICE ROADS OF UNIT 1 WITH INTERSTATE 15 AND IVANPAH DRY LAKE RACETRACK IN THE BACKGROUND

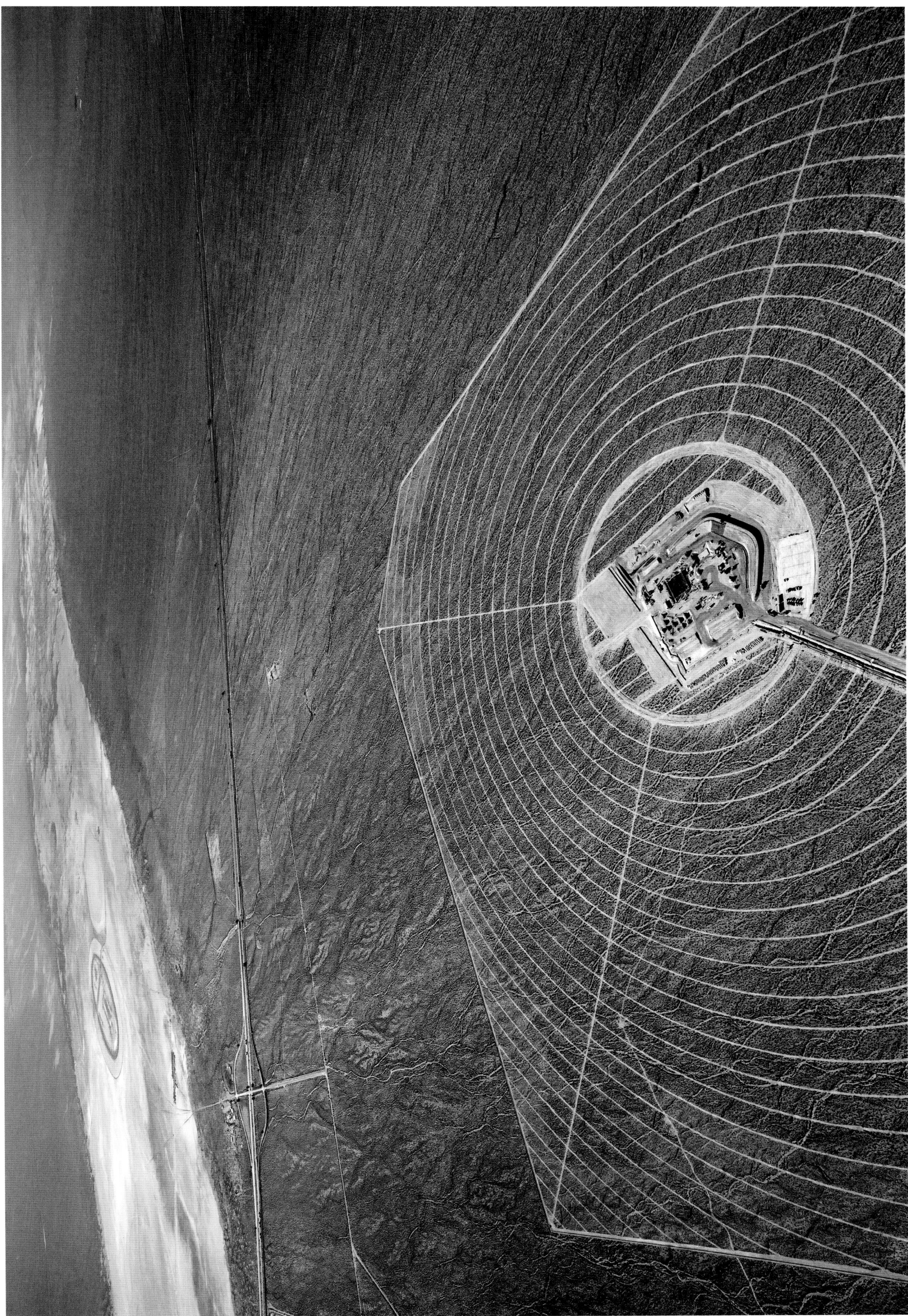

#5240, 6 JANUARY 2012

HELIOSTAT PYLON STACKS NEAR SERVICE ROADS OF UNIT 2

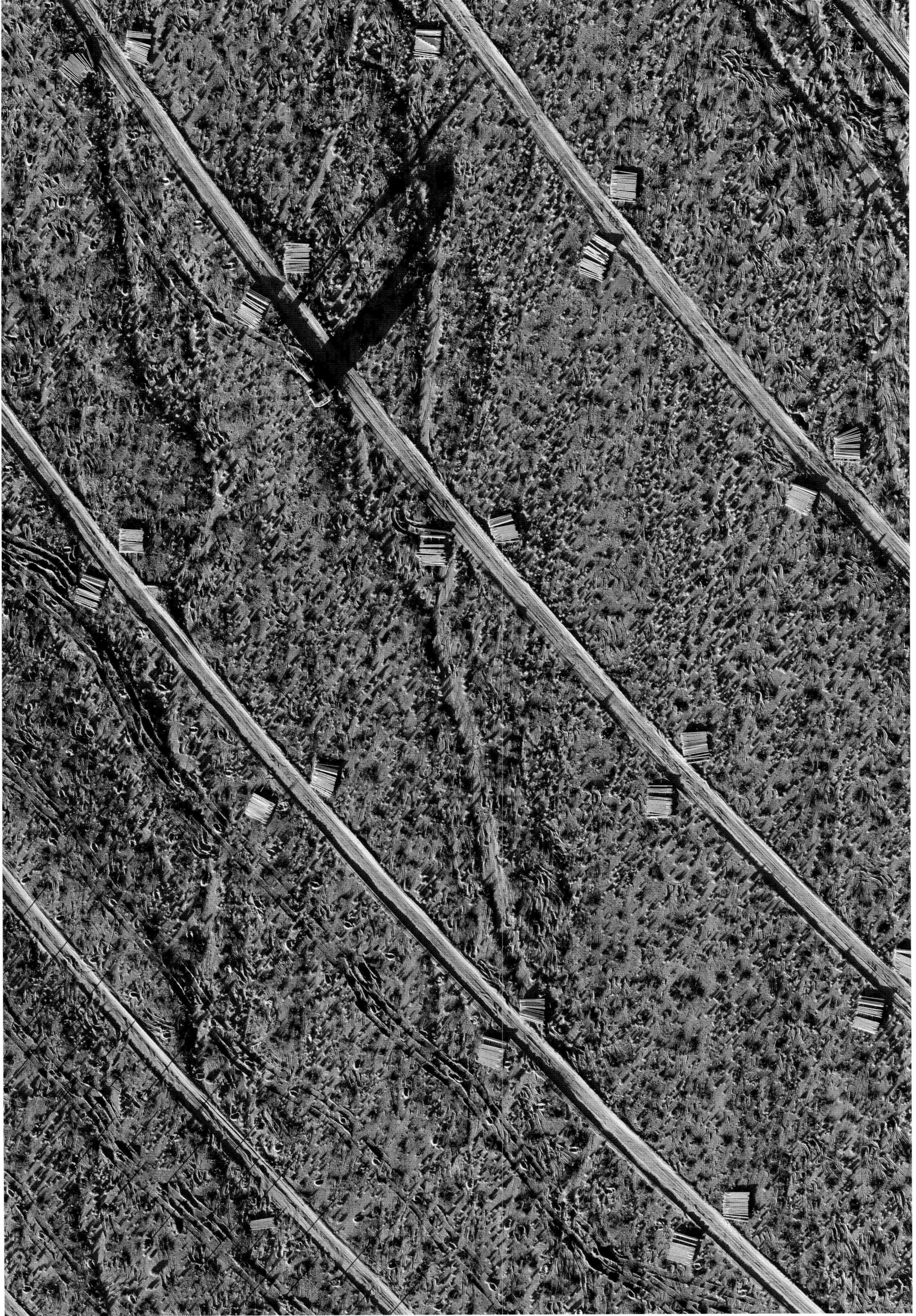

#6462, 2 JUNE 2012

SERVICE ROADS, OTHER VEHICLE TRACKS, AND PYLON SHADOWS PRIOR TO HELIOSTAT INSTALLATION

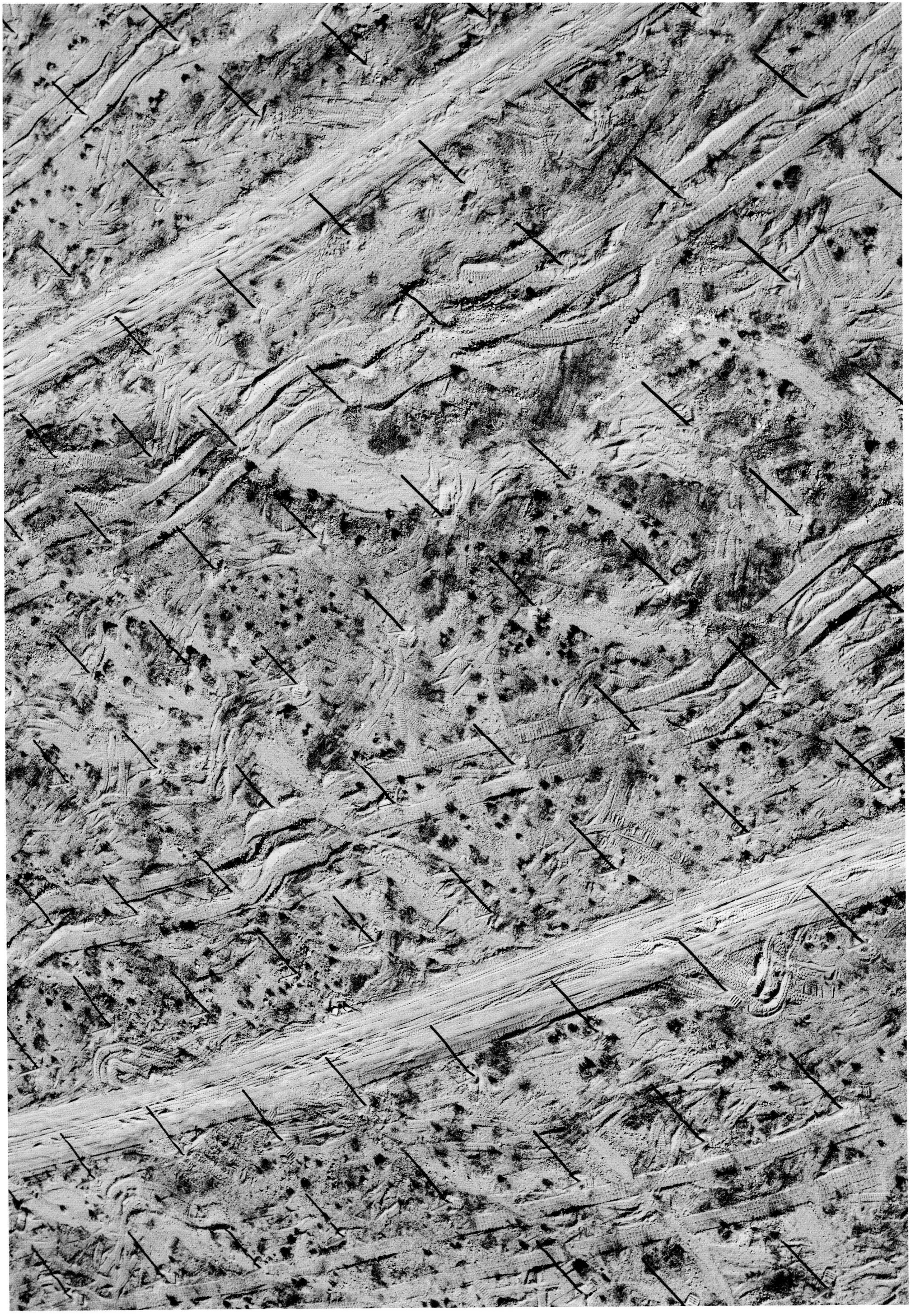

#6126, 11 APRIL 2012

BOUNDARY OF UNIT 3 SKIRTS A HILL TO THE WEST OF THE PROJECT

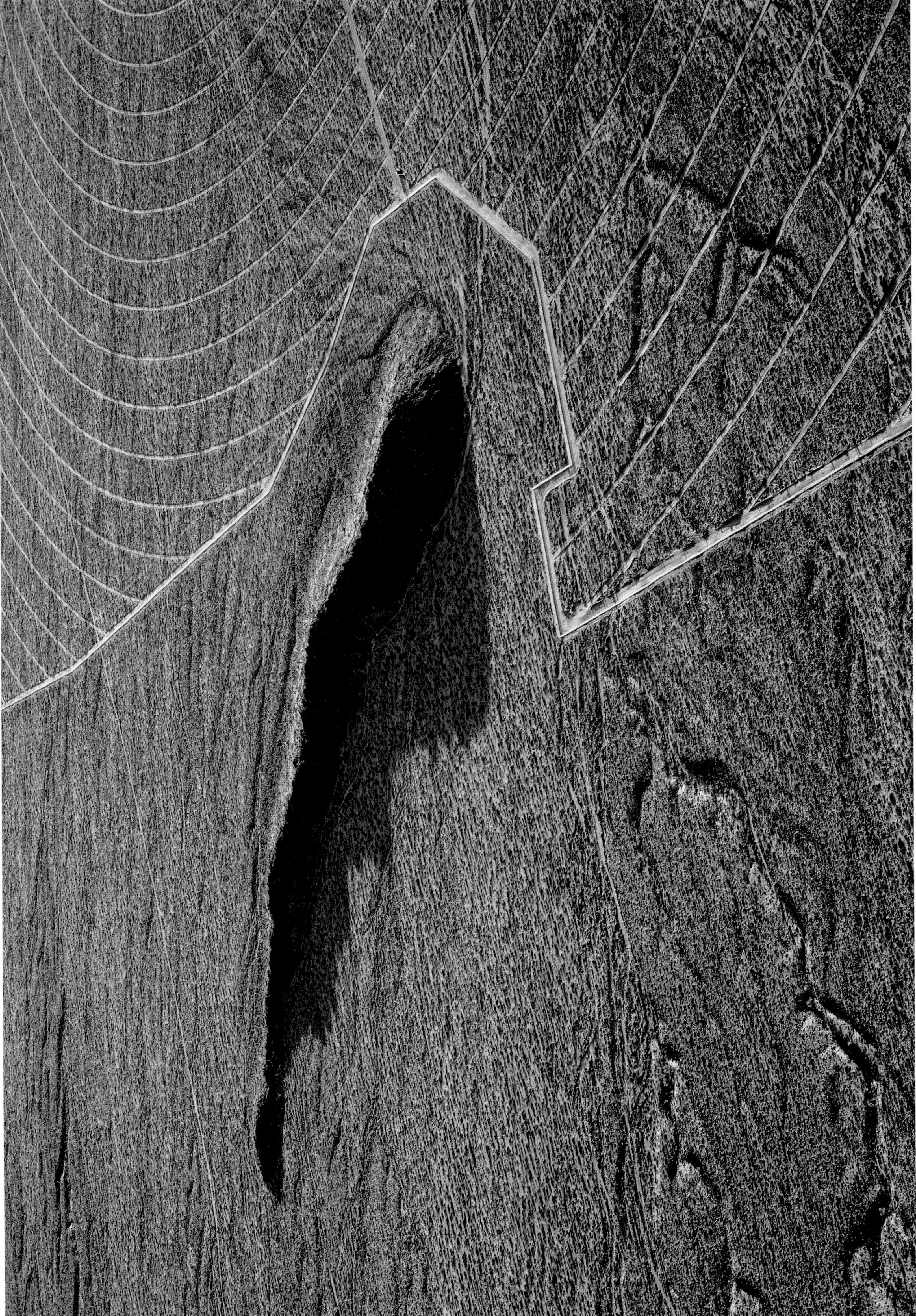

#3696, 28 JULY 2011

PAD PREPARATION FOR SUBSTATION WITH UNIT 1 CONSTRUCTION IN THE DISTANCE

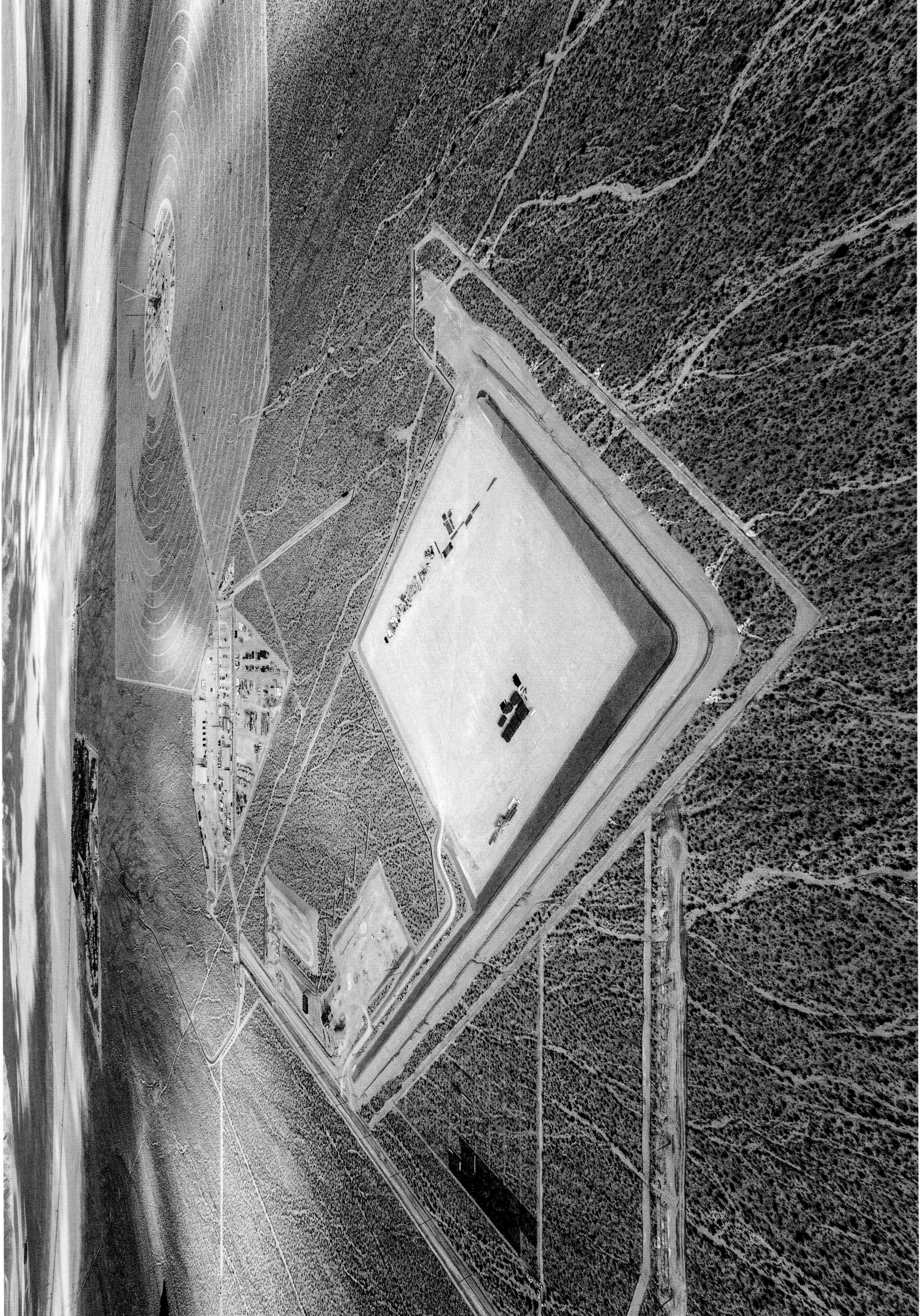

#5650, 6 JANUARY 2012

DETAIL OF UNIT 2 POWER BLOCK CONSTRUCTION

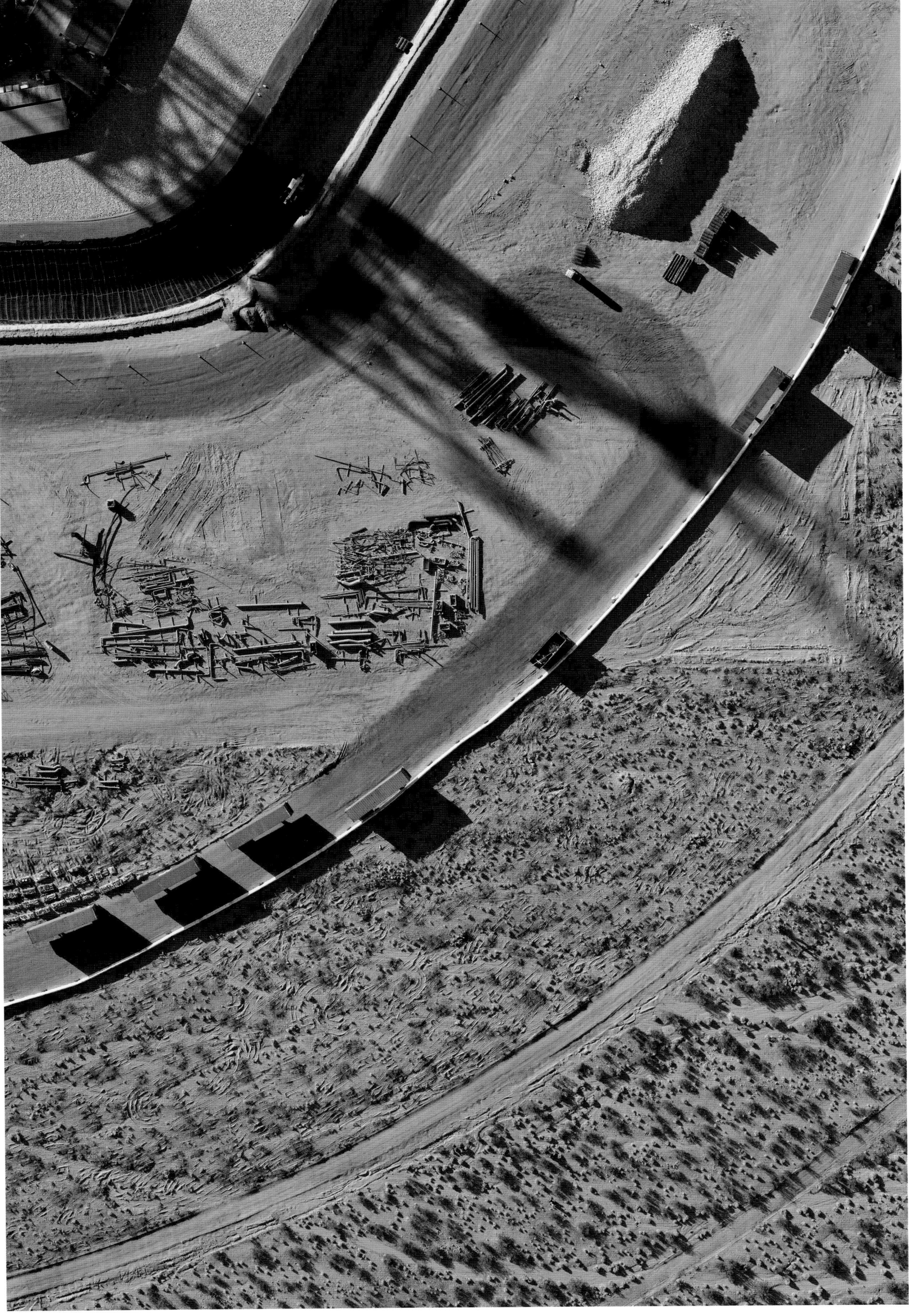

#6279, 11 APRIL 2012

DETAIL OF UNIT 2 POWER BLOCK CONSTRUCTION

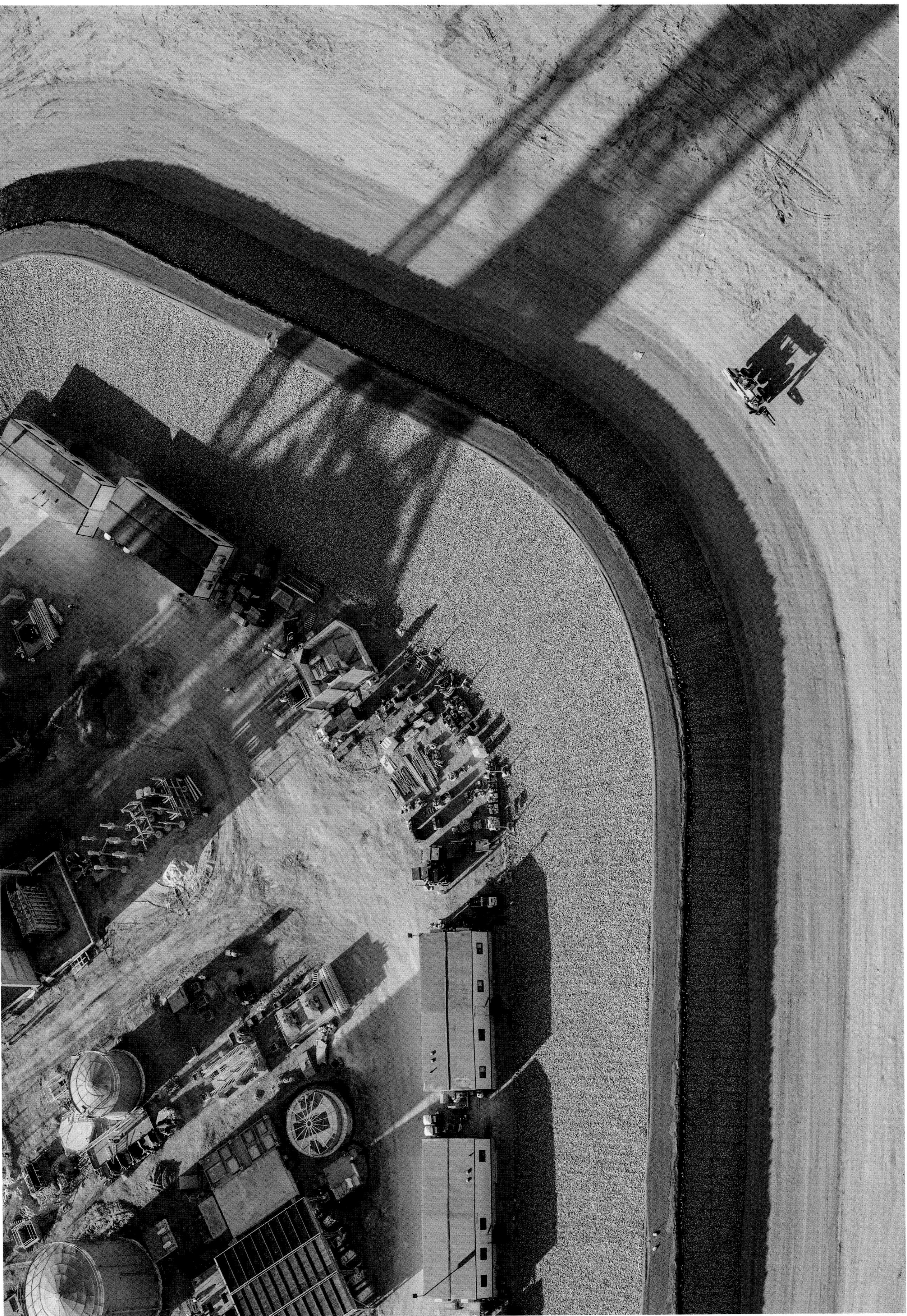

#6163, 11 APRIL 2012

UNIT 2 POWER BLOCK CONSTRUCTION WITH TOWER, CRANE, AND VEHICLES OF CONSTRUCTION WORKERS

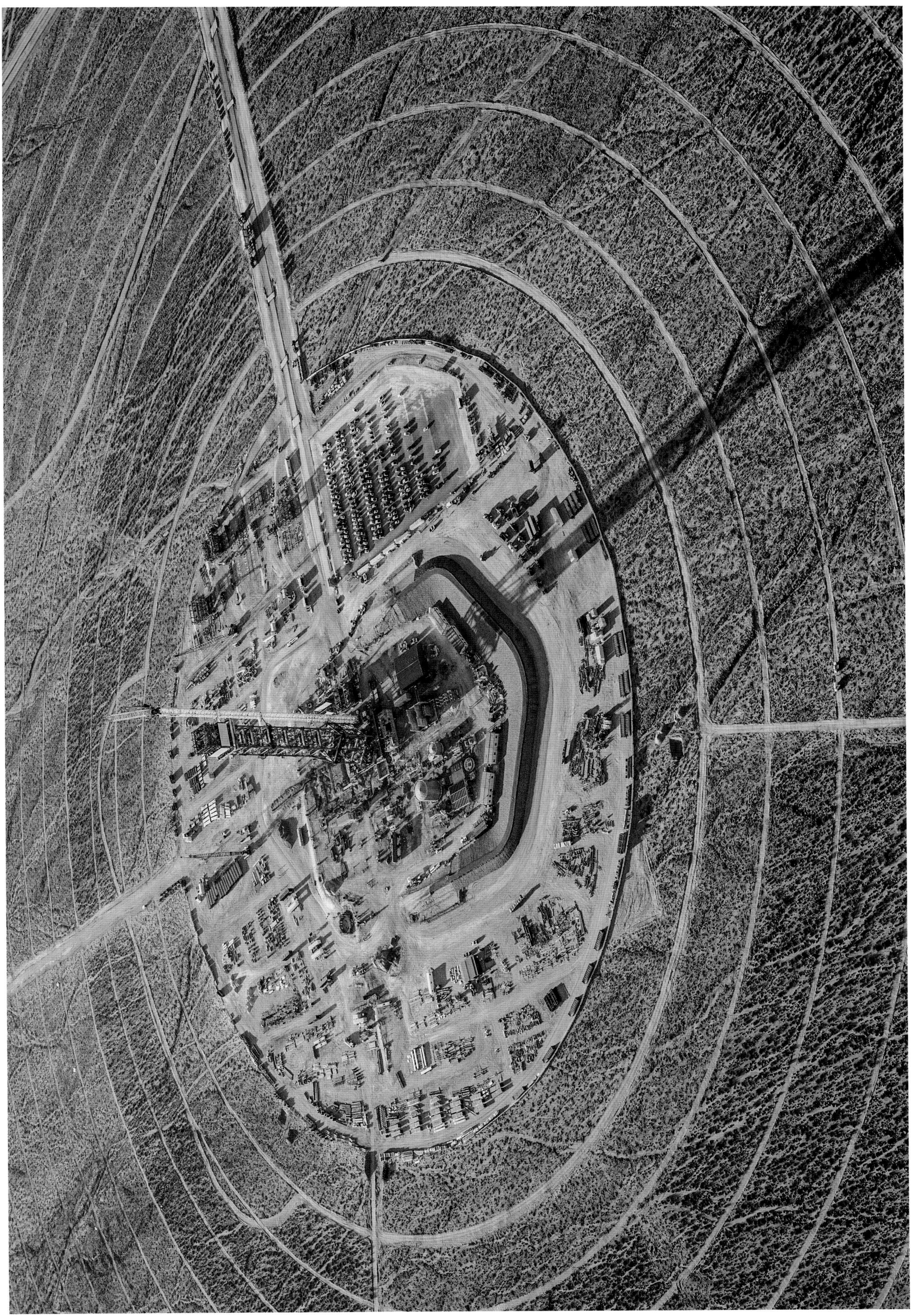

#5396, 6 JANUARY 2012

ASSEMBLED HELIOSTATS (MIRROR PAIRS ON FRAMES) AWAIT INSTALLATION OUTSIDE THE HELIOSTAT ASSEMBLY BUILDING

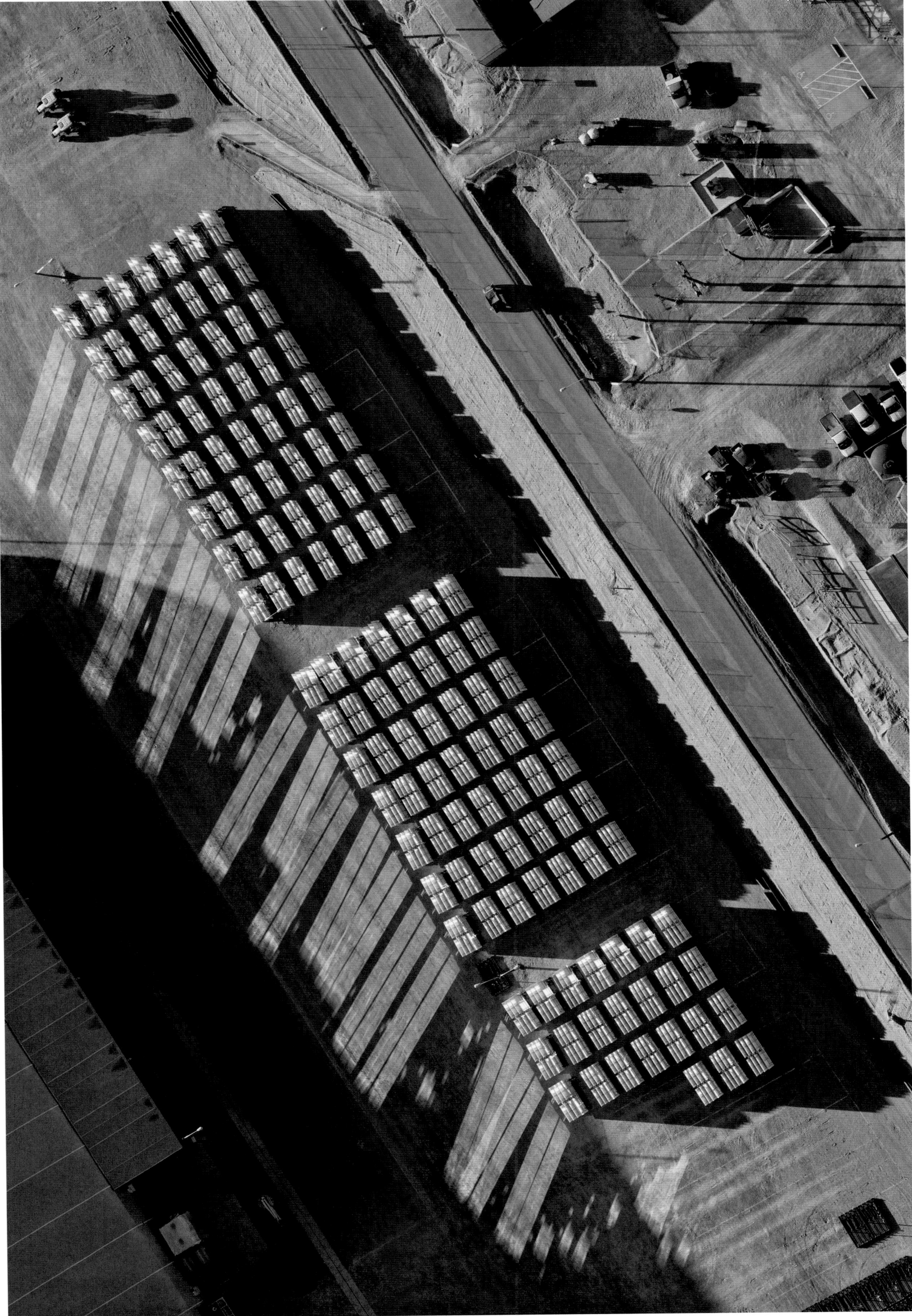

#4904, 6 JANUARY 2012

INITIAL HELIOSTAT (MIRROR) INSTALLATION ON WEST SIDE OF UNIT 1

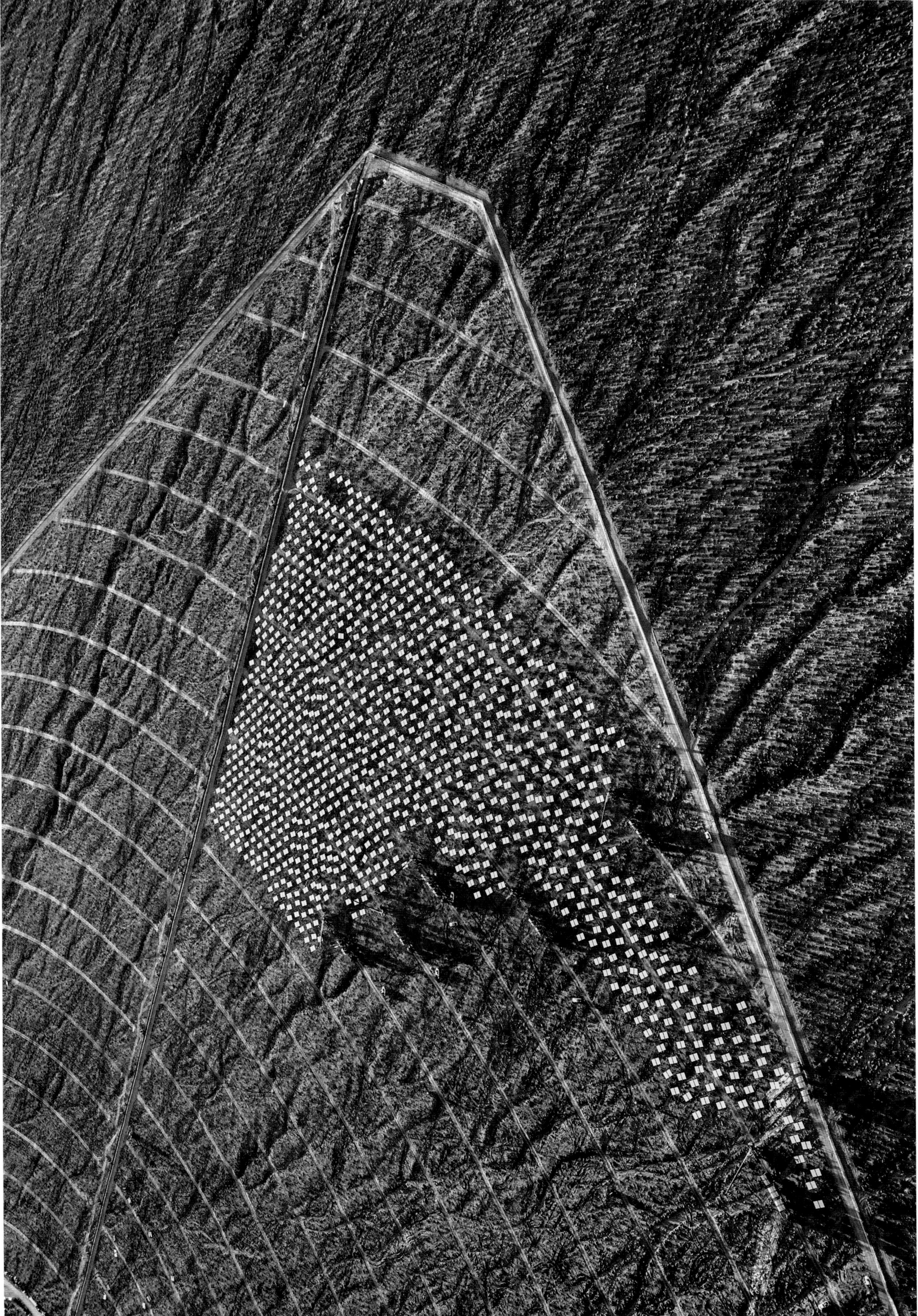

#8695, 27 OCTOBER 2012

A HILL FORMATION RISES ABOVE THE SURROUNDING ALLUVIAL SLOPE AT THE EASTERN BOUNDARIES OF UNITS 2 AND 3

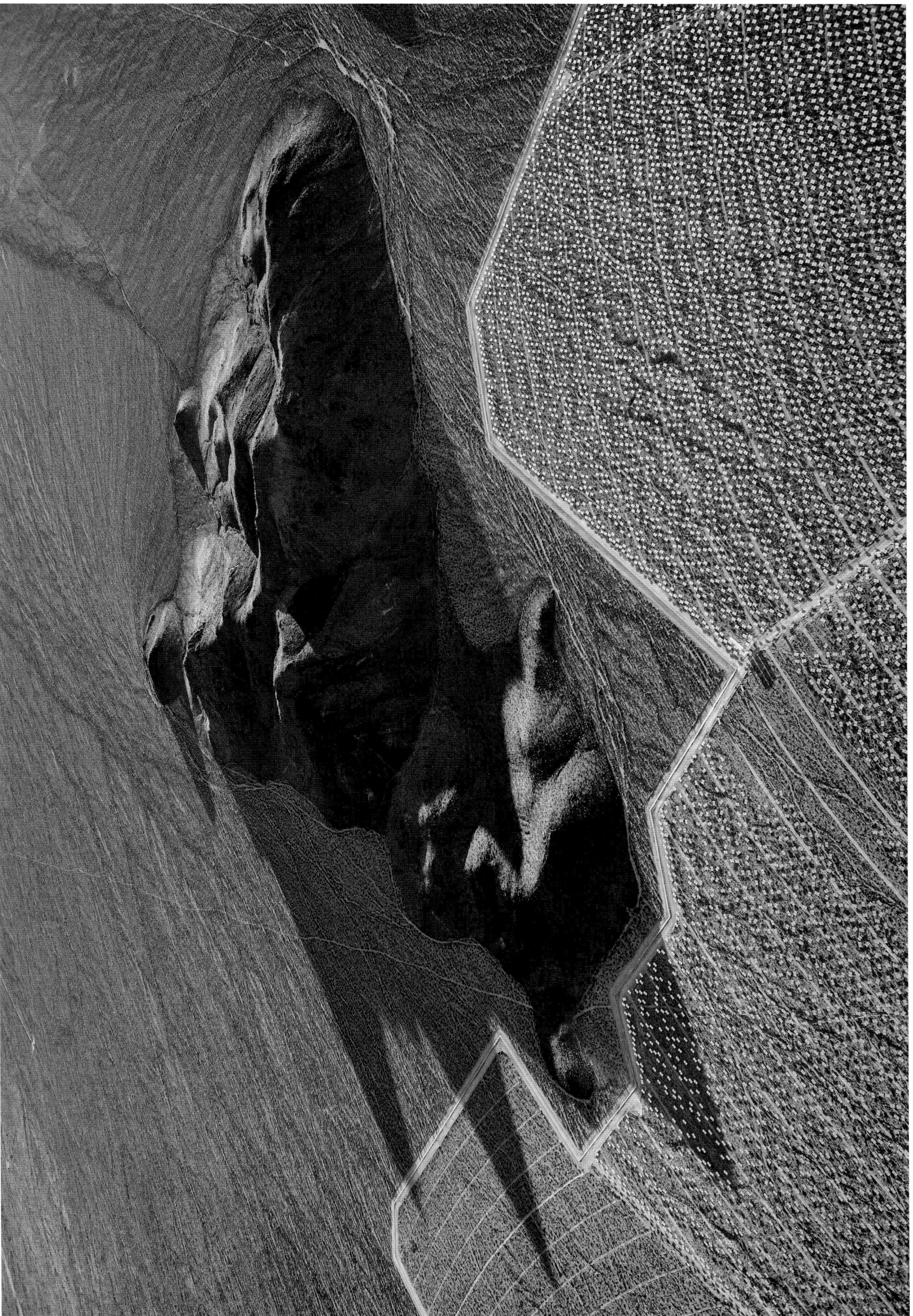

#6721, 2 JUNE 2012

HELIOSTATS NEAR PROJECT BOUNDARY OF UNIT 1

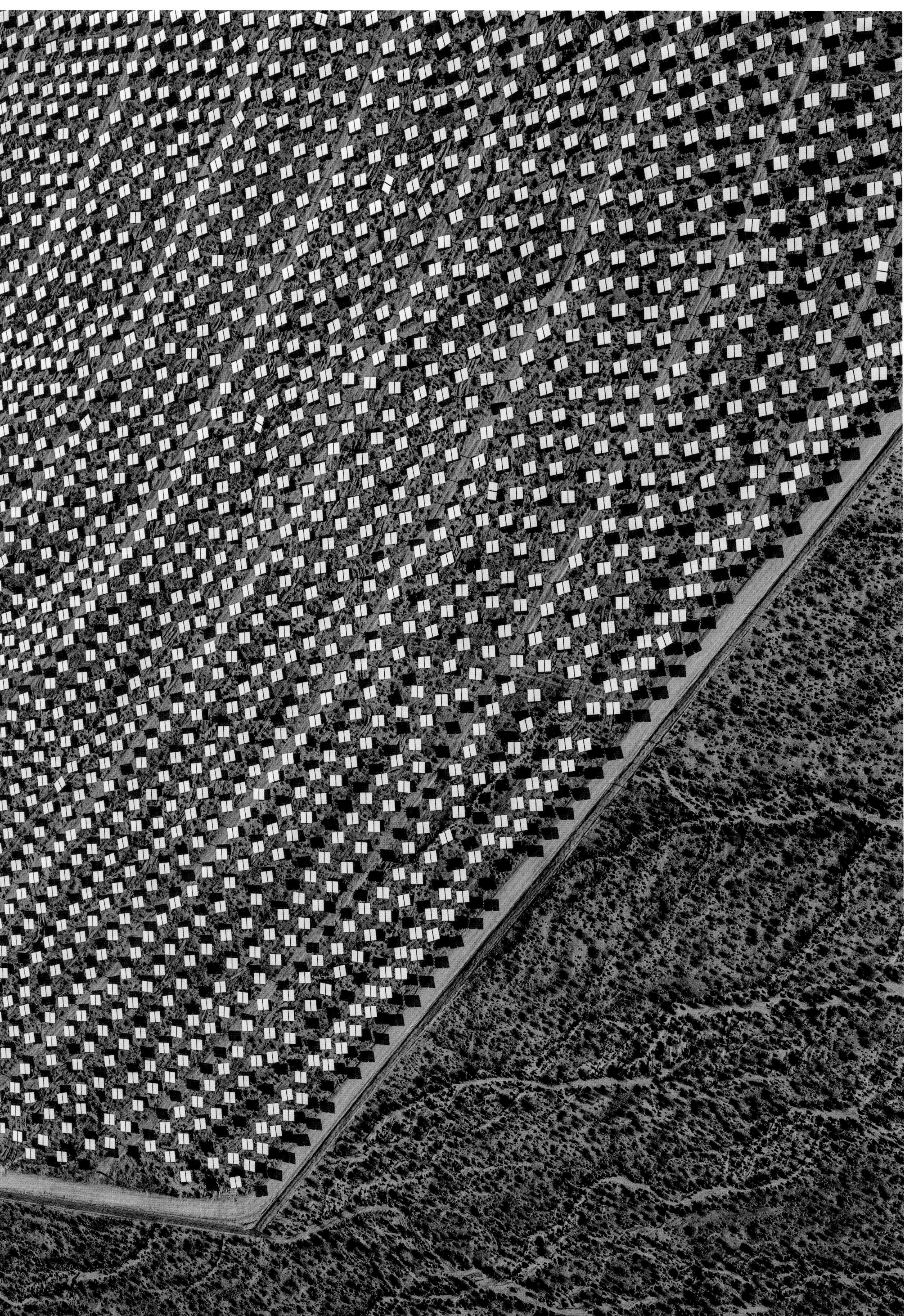

#6425, 2 JUNE 2012

INSTALLED HELIOSTATS IN HORIZONTAL OR “SAFE MODE”

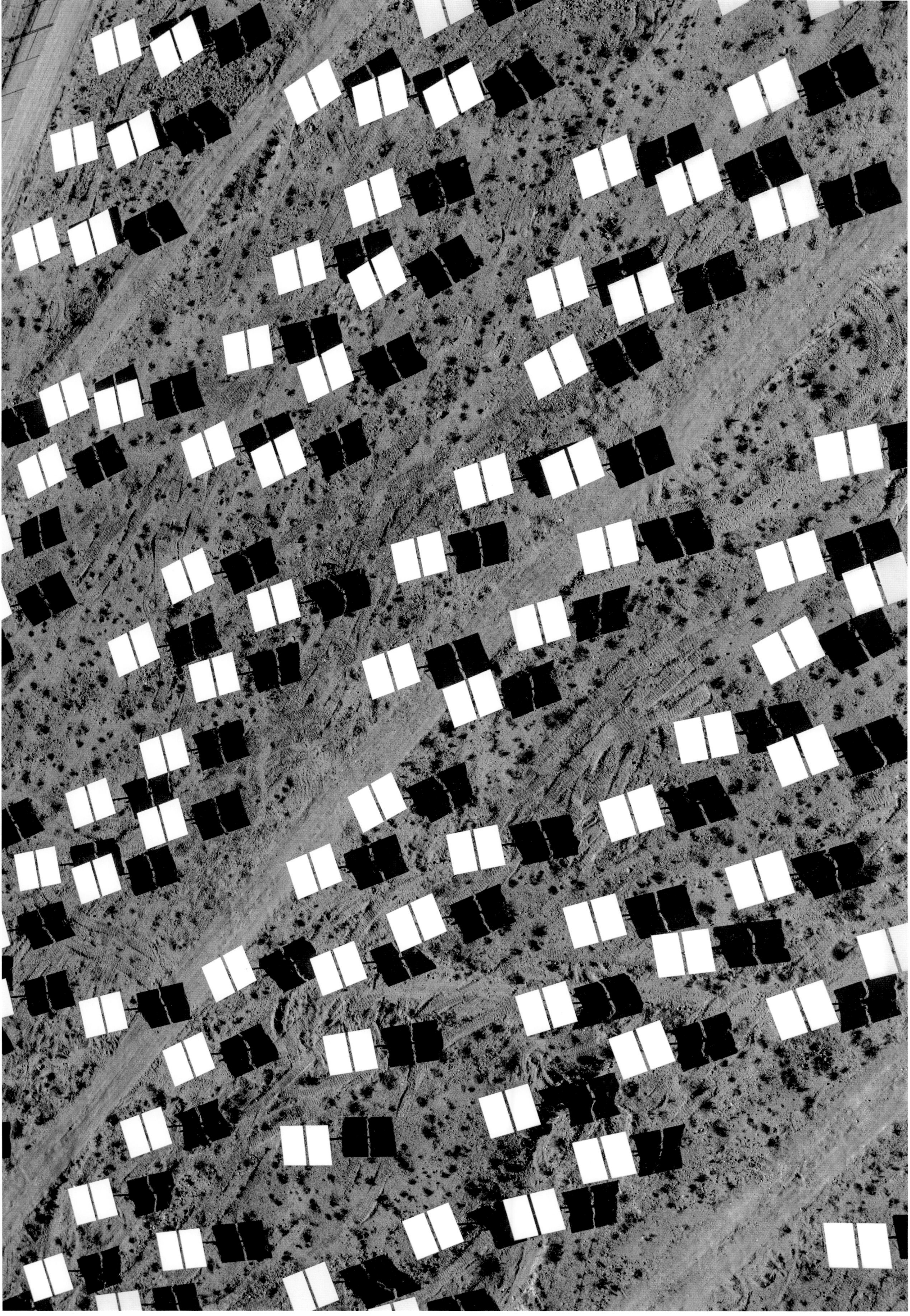

#7626, 4 JUNE 2012

WORKERS INSTALL A HELIOSTAT FOR UNIT 1 WITH MOUNTAINS REFLECTED IN ITS MIRRORS

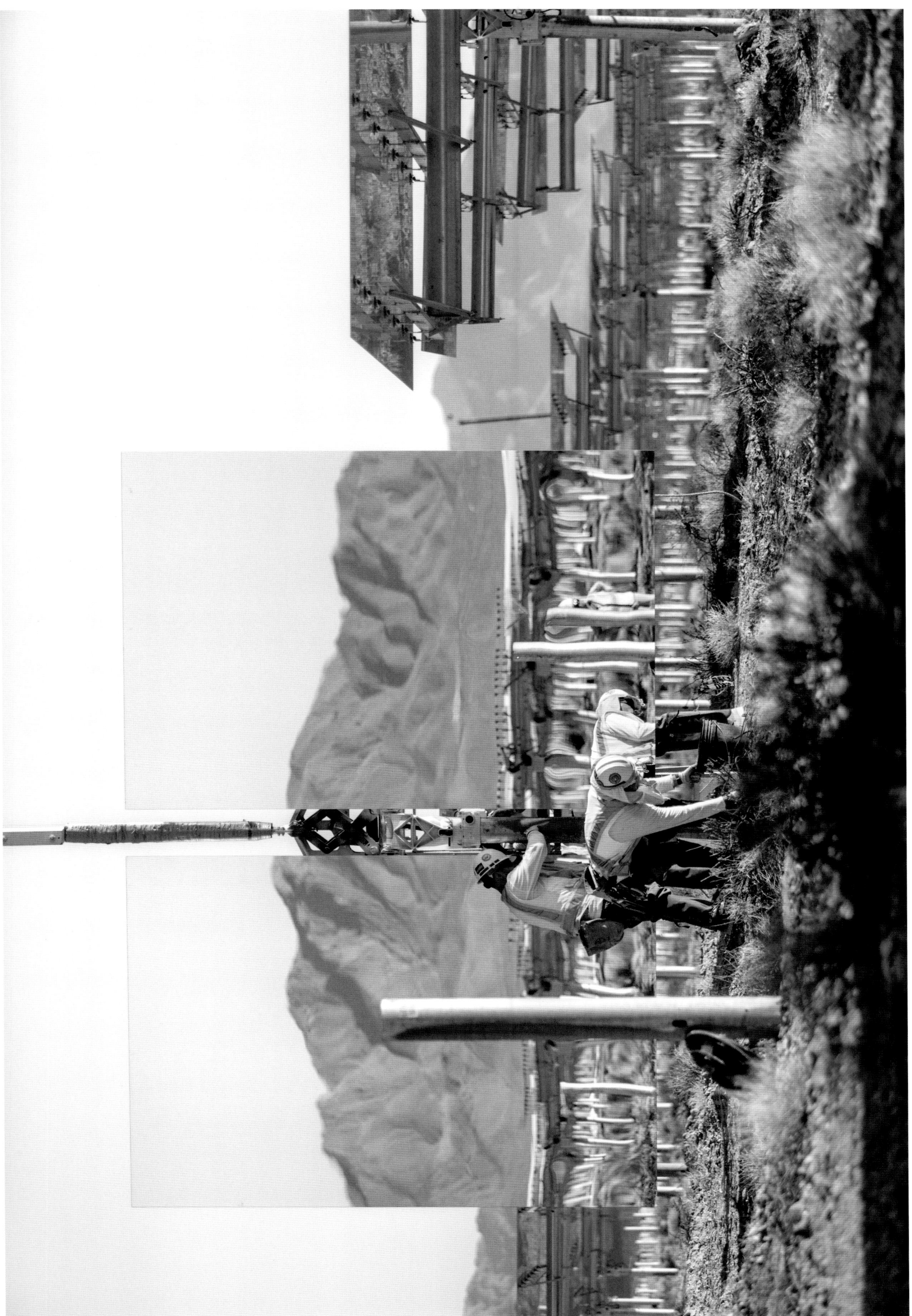

#6048, 11 APRIL 2012

VIEW SOUTH OF UNIT 1 CONSTRUCTION WITH UNIT 2 IN THE FOREGROUND

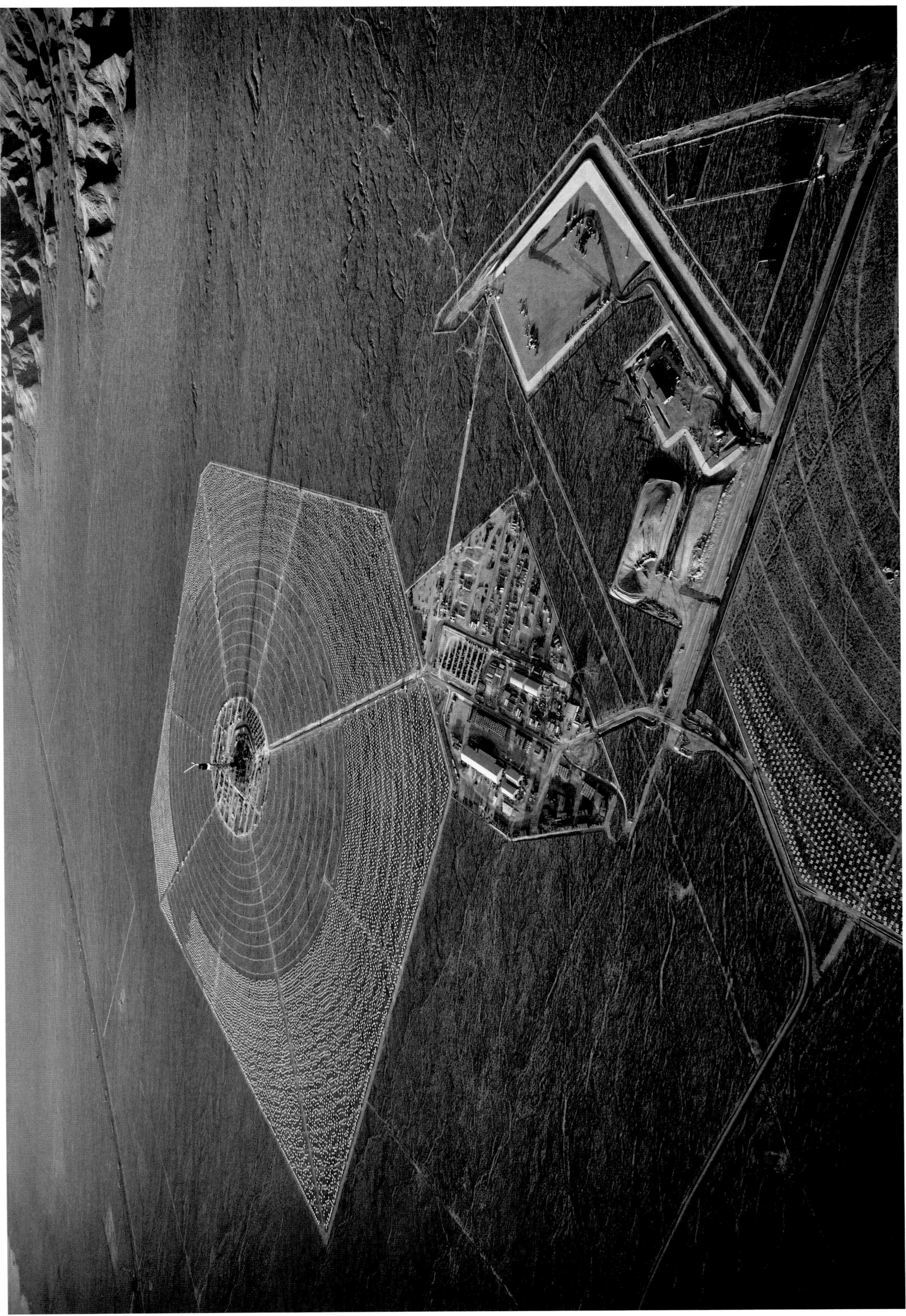

#11250, 4 SEPTEMBER 2013

THE CASINO COMMUNITY OF PRIMM, NEVADA, WITH IVANPAH IN THE DISTANCE TO THE SOUTHWEST

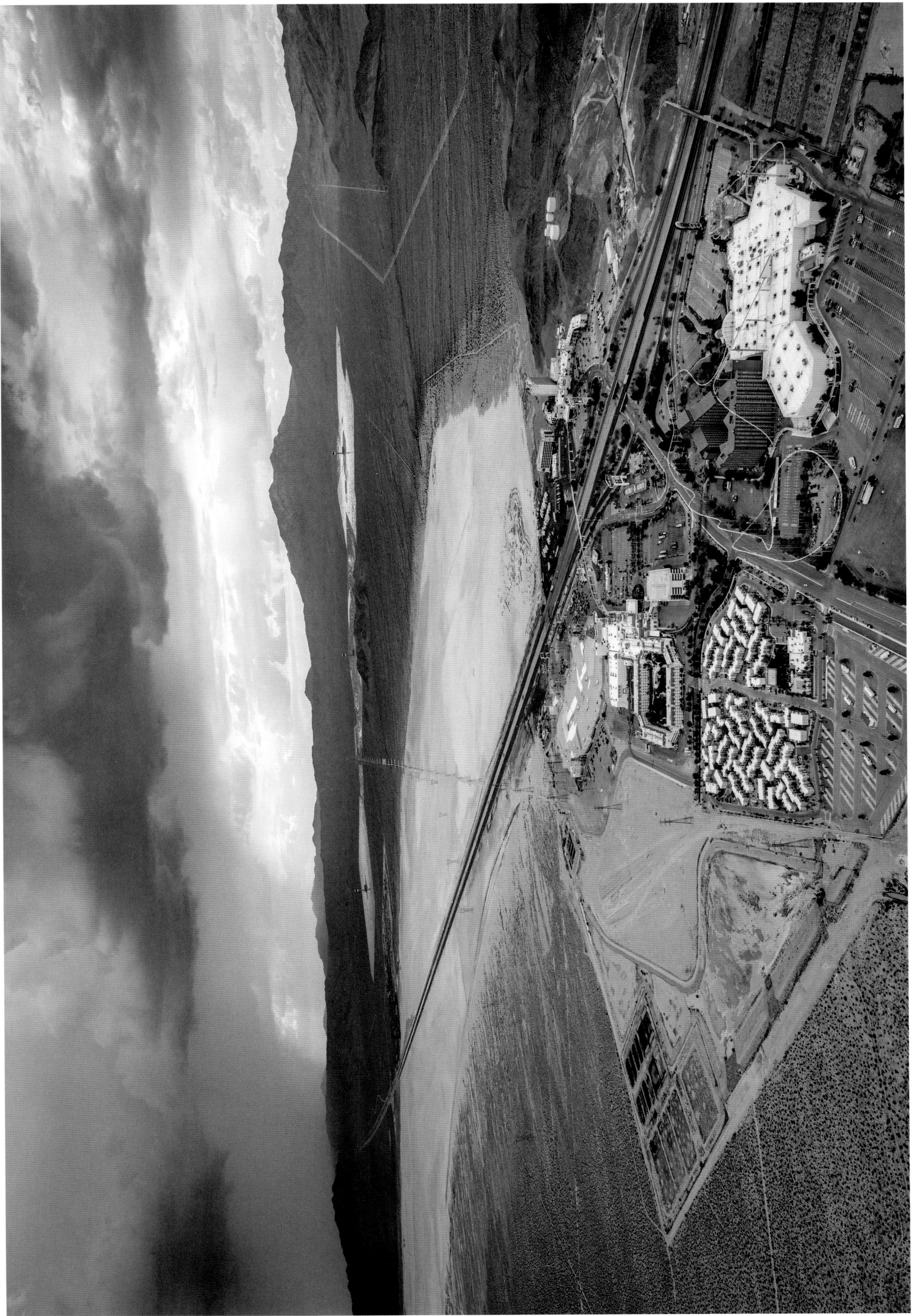

#7986, 5 JUNE 2012

DIRT RACETRACK OF IVANPAH DRY LAKE BED WITH INTERSTATE 15, GOLF RESORT, IVANPAH, AND CLARK MOUNTAIN IN THE DISTANCE

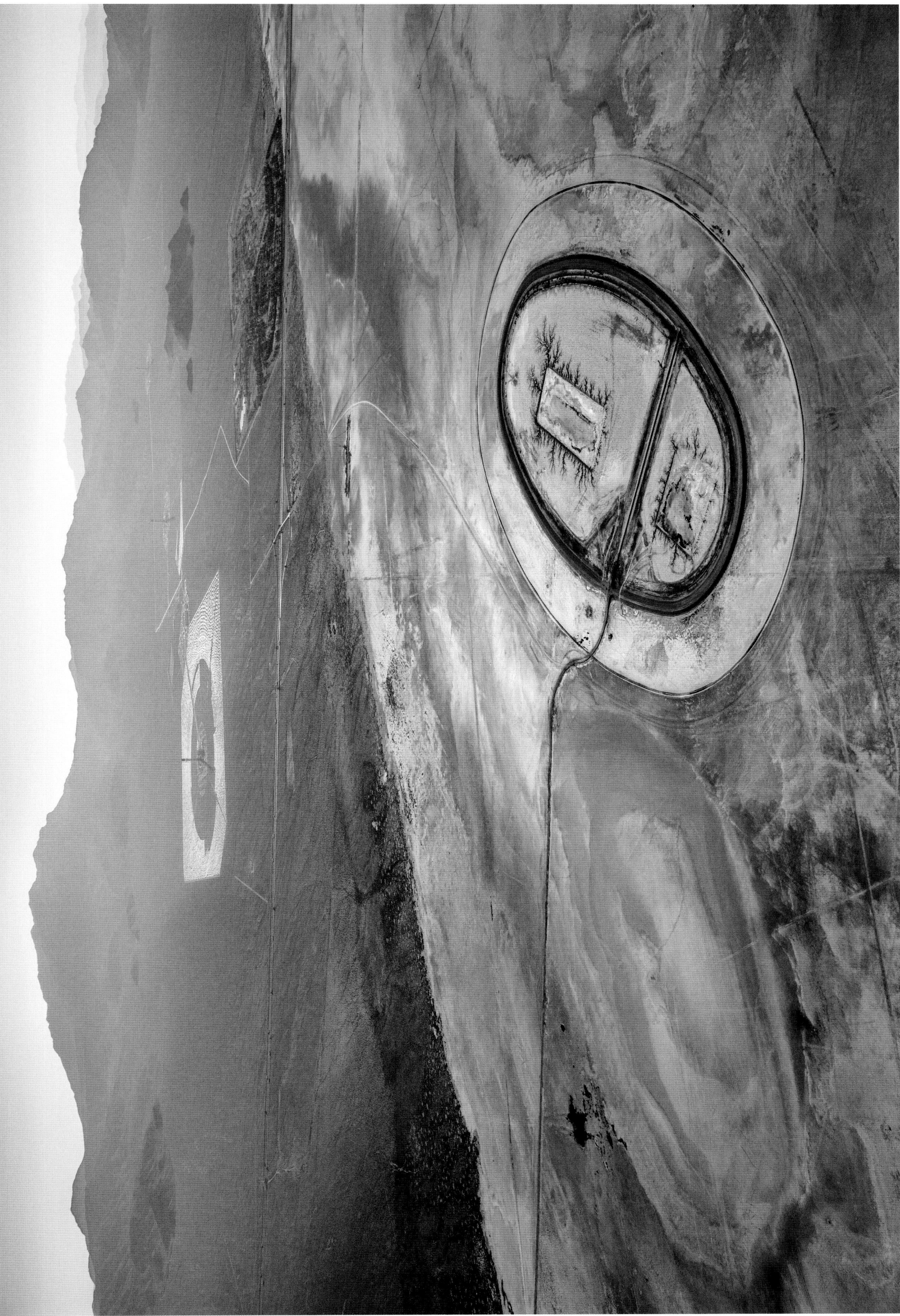

#8583, 27 OCTOBER 2012

TOWER, POWER BLOCK, AND FIELD OF UNIT 3 PRIOR TO HELIOSTAT INSTALLATION

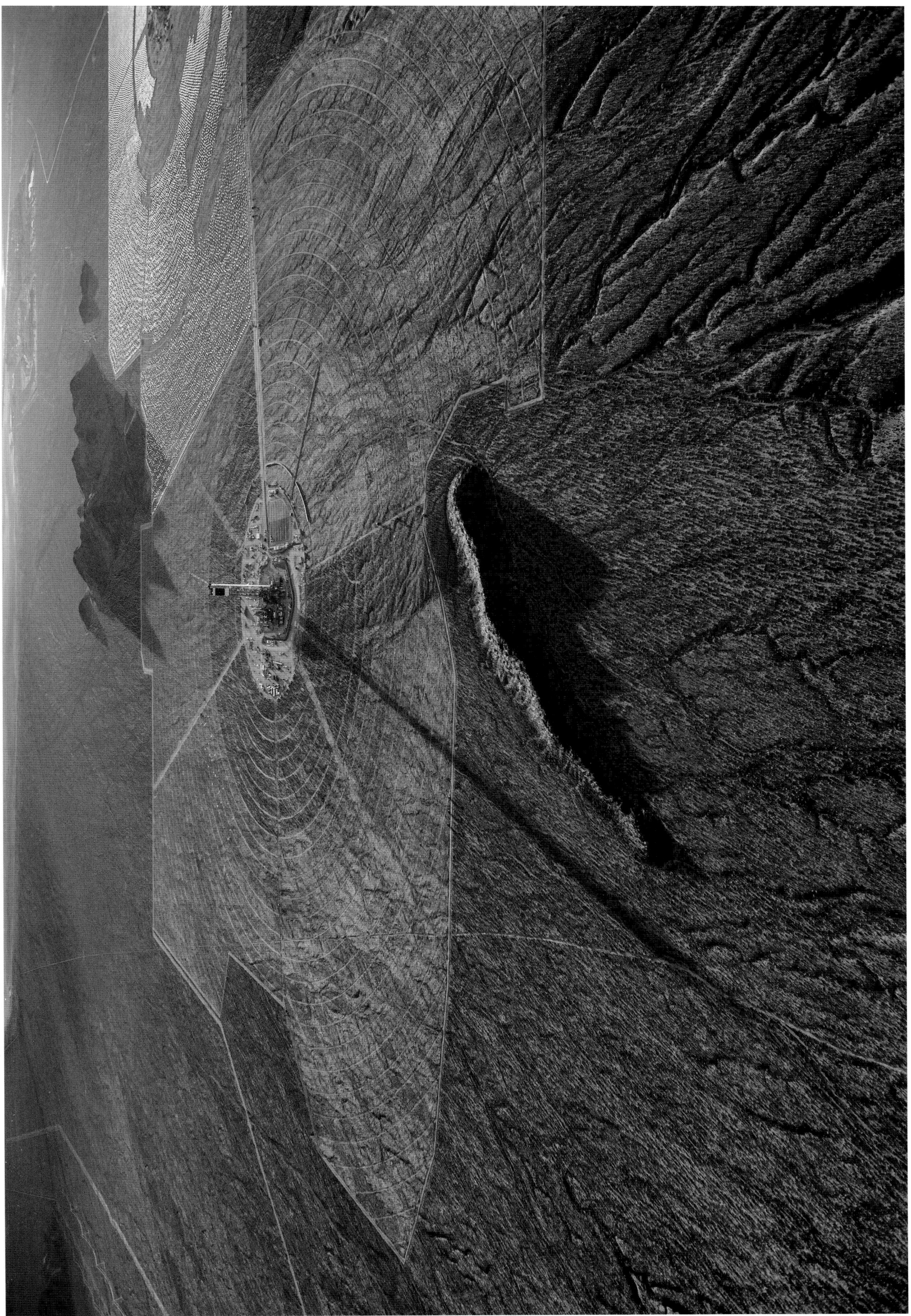

#9499, 21 MARCH 2013

A HILL FORMATION RISES ABOVE THE ALLUVIAL SLOPE AT THE EASTERN BOUNDARIES OF UNITS 2 AND 3 WITH HELIOSTAT INSTALLATION COMPLETE

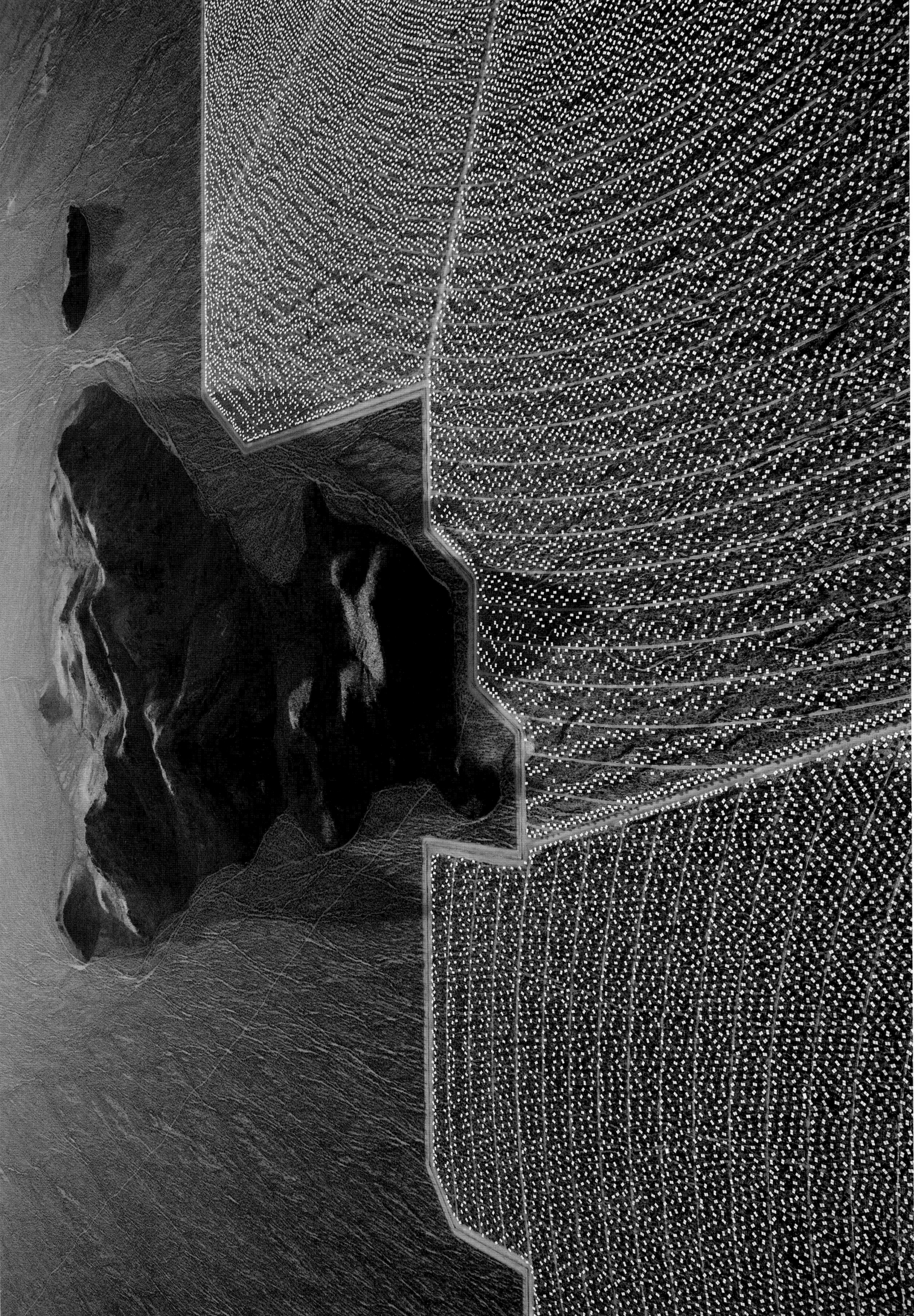

#10006, 25 JUNE 2013

HELIOSTATS NEAR THE BOUNDARY OF UNIT 3

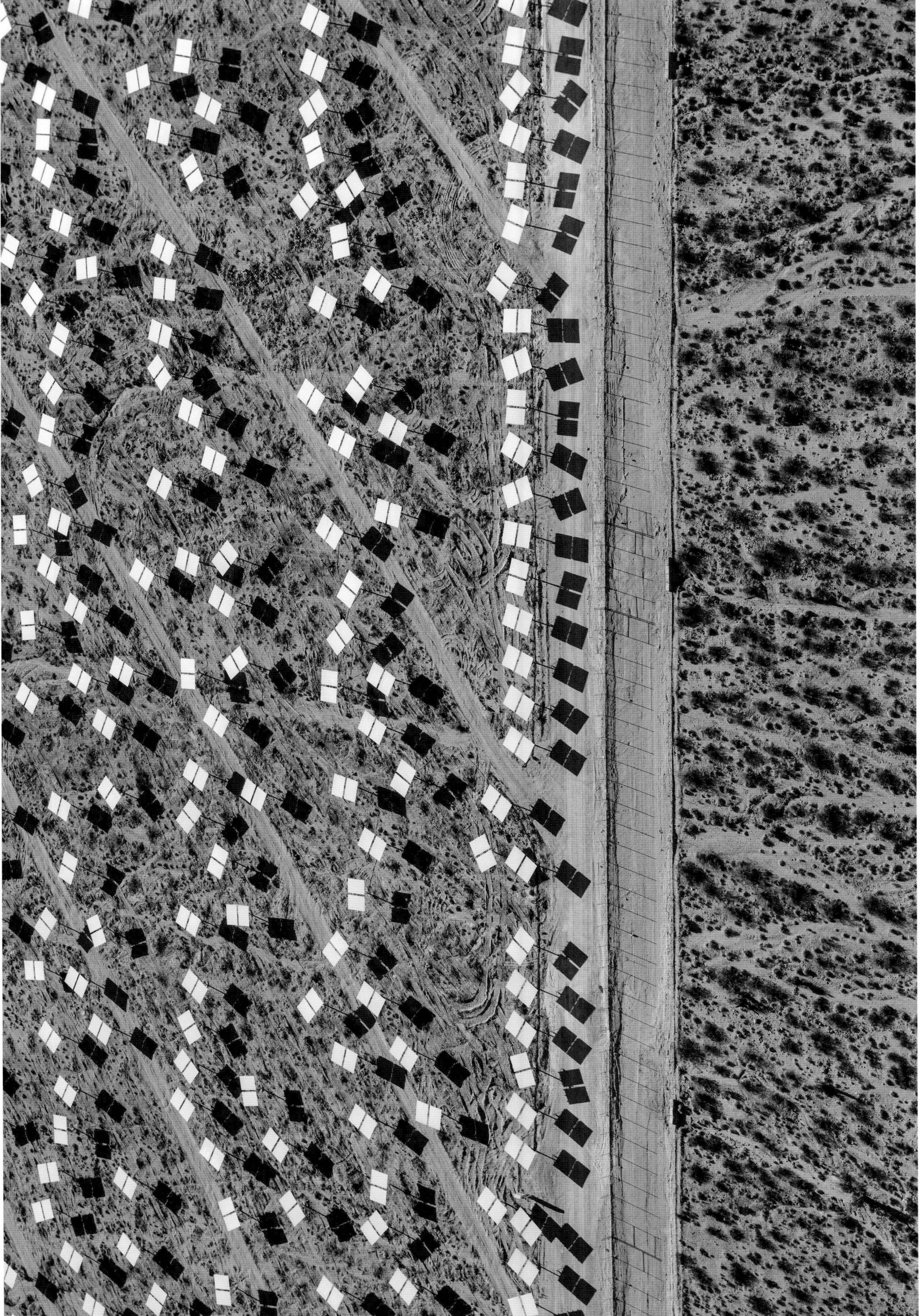

#9637, 21 MARCH 2013

HELIOSTAT INSTALLATION ADJACENT TO UNIT 1 POWER BLOCK

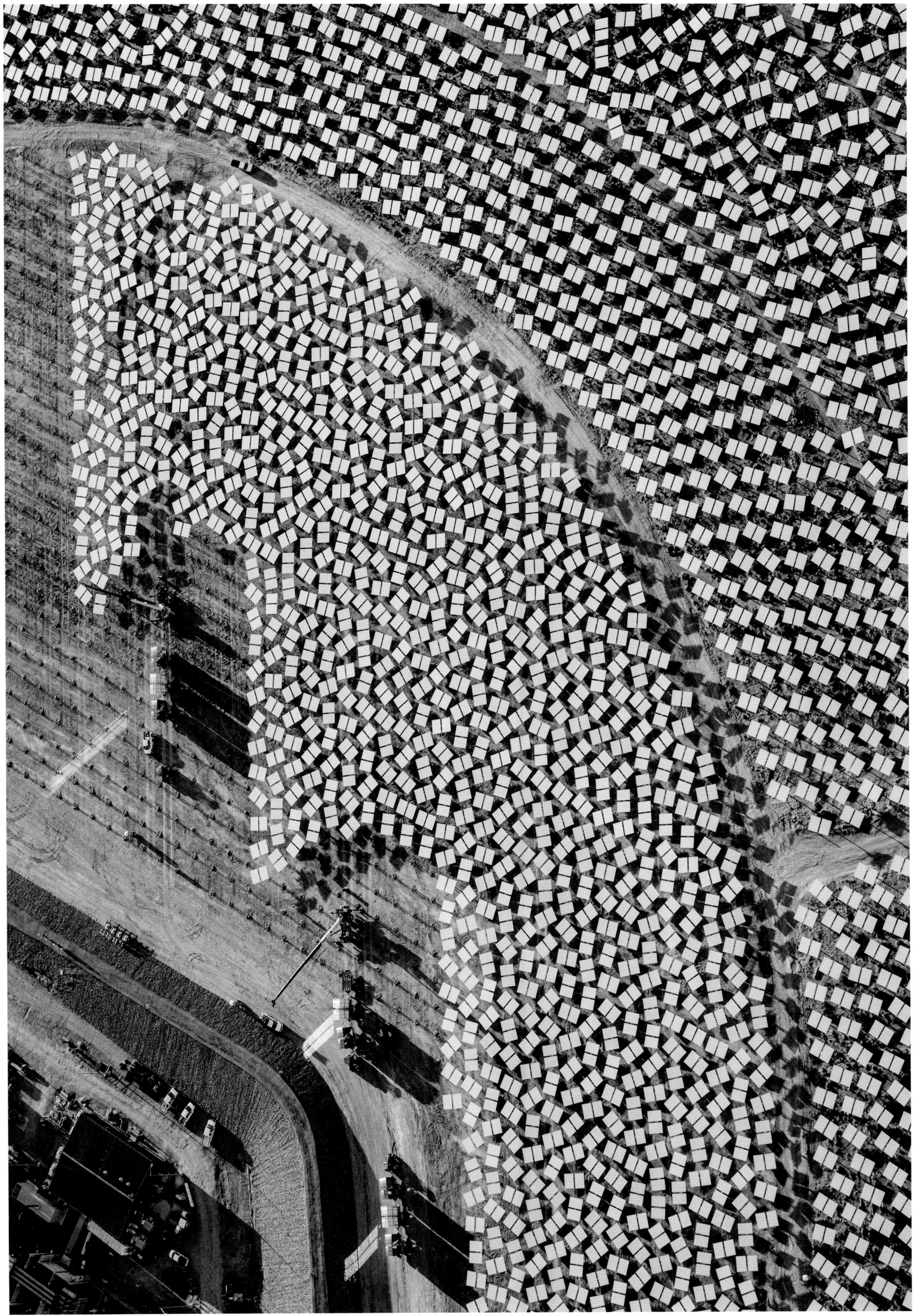

#6655, 2 JUNE 2012

INTERSTATE 15 RUNNING NORTH TOWARD PRIMM AND LAS VEGAS, NEVADA, WITH IVANPAH IN THE DISTANCE

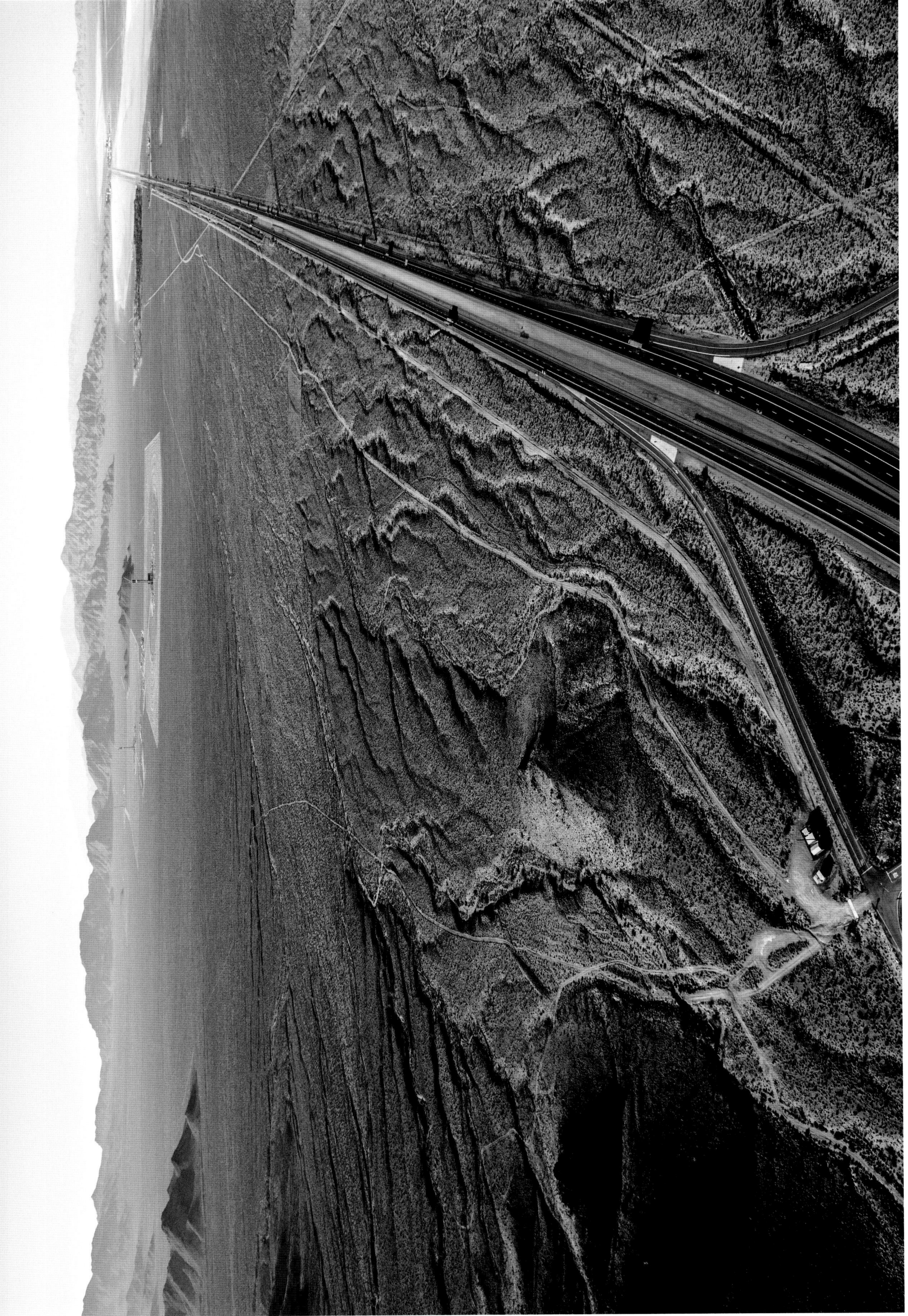

#8502, 27 OCTOBER 2012

VIEW NORTH OF IVANPAH UNITS 1, 2, AND 3 AT SUNRISE

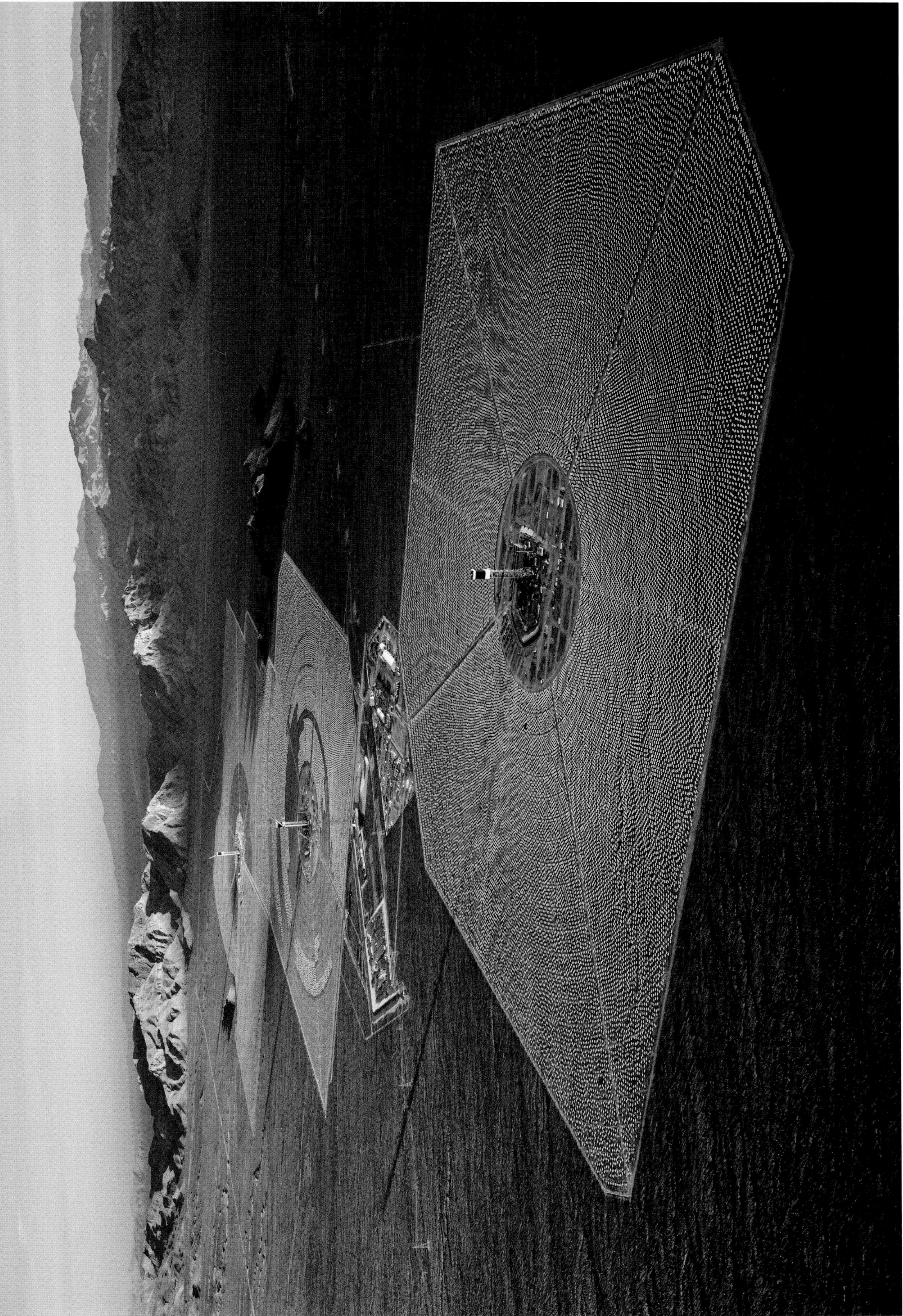

#8796, 27 OCTOBER 2012

TOWER AND POWER BLOCK SURROUNDED BY HELIOSTATS OF UNIT 1

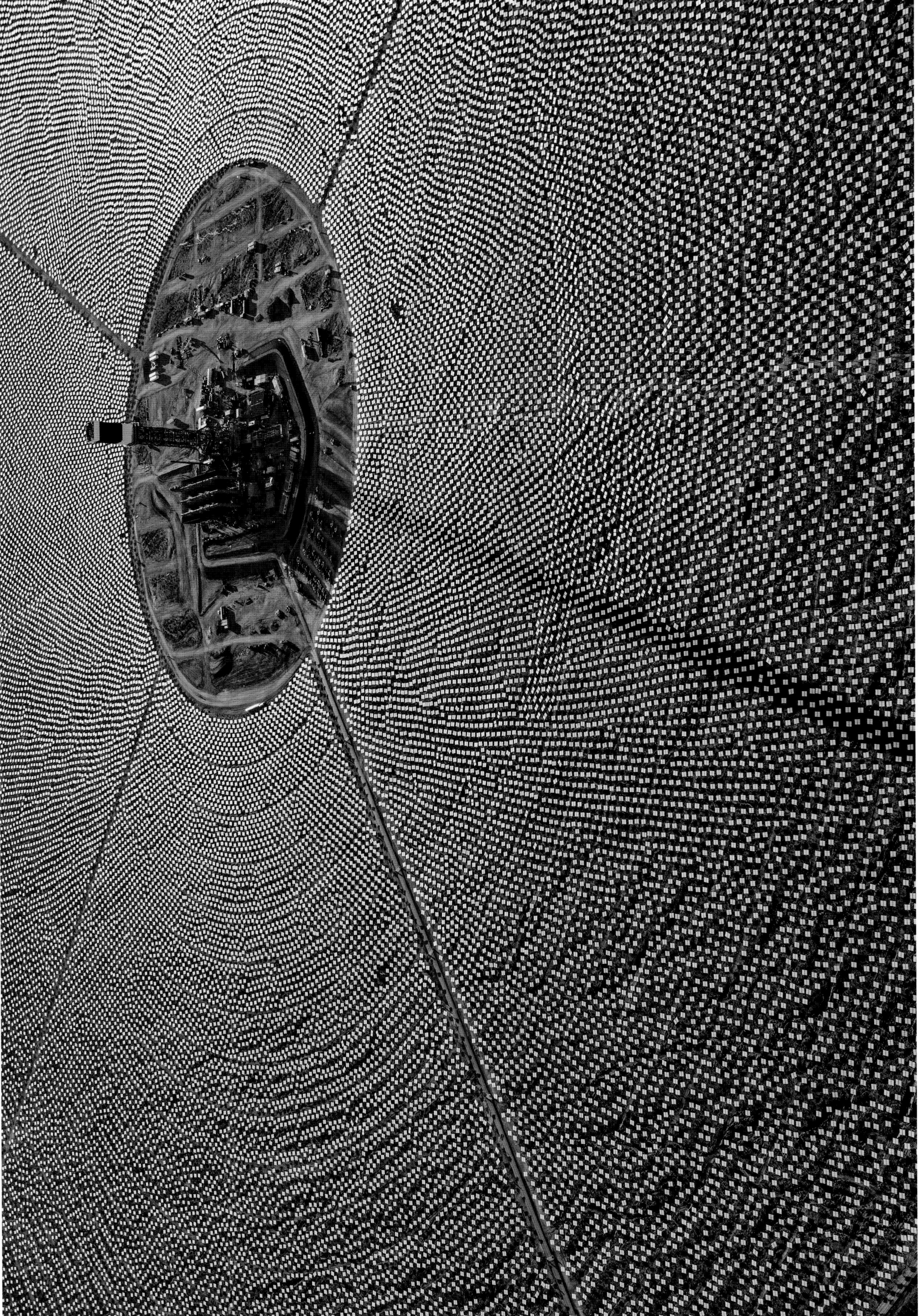

#10099, 25 JUNE 2013

PYLON SHADOWS NEAR UNIT 2 POWER BLOCK

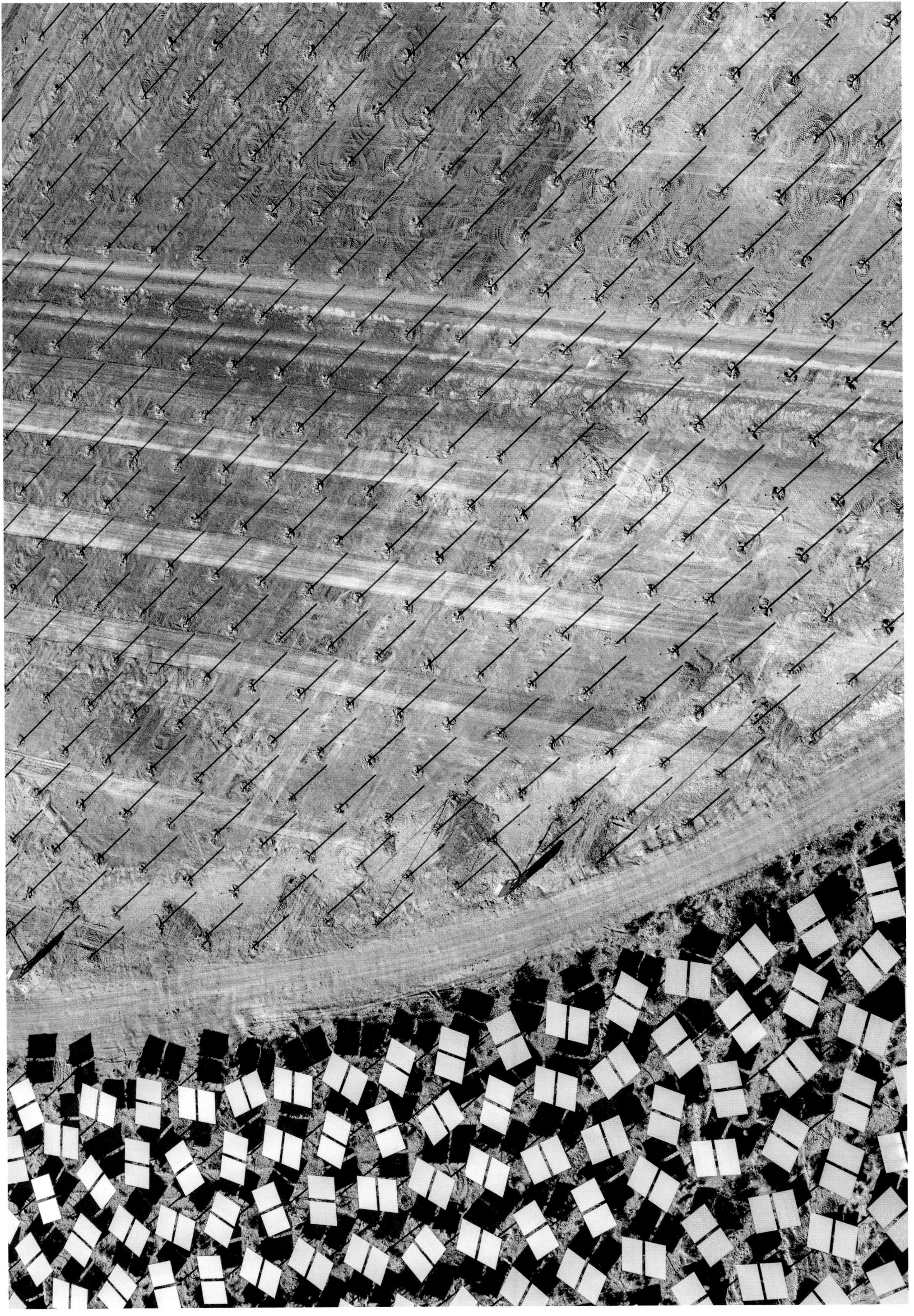

#5237, 6 JANUARY 2012

“HEAD START” NURSERY AREA FOR JUVENILE DESERT TORTOISES ADJACENT TO FUTURE SUBSTATION SITE

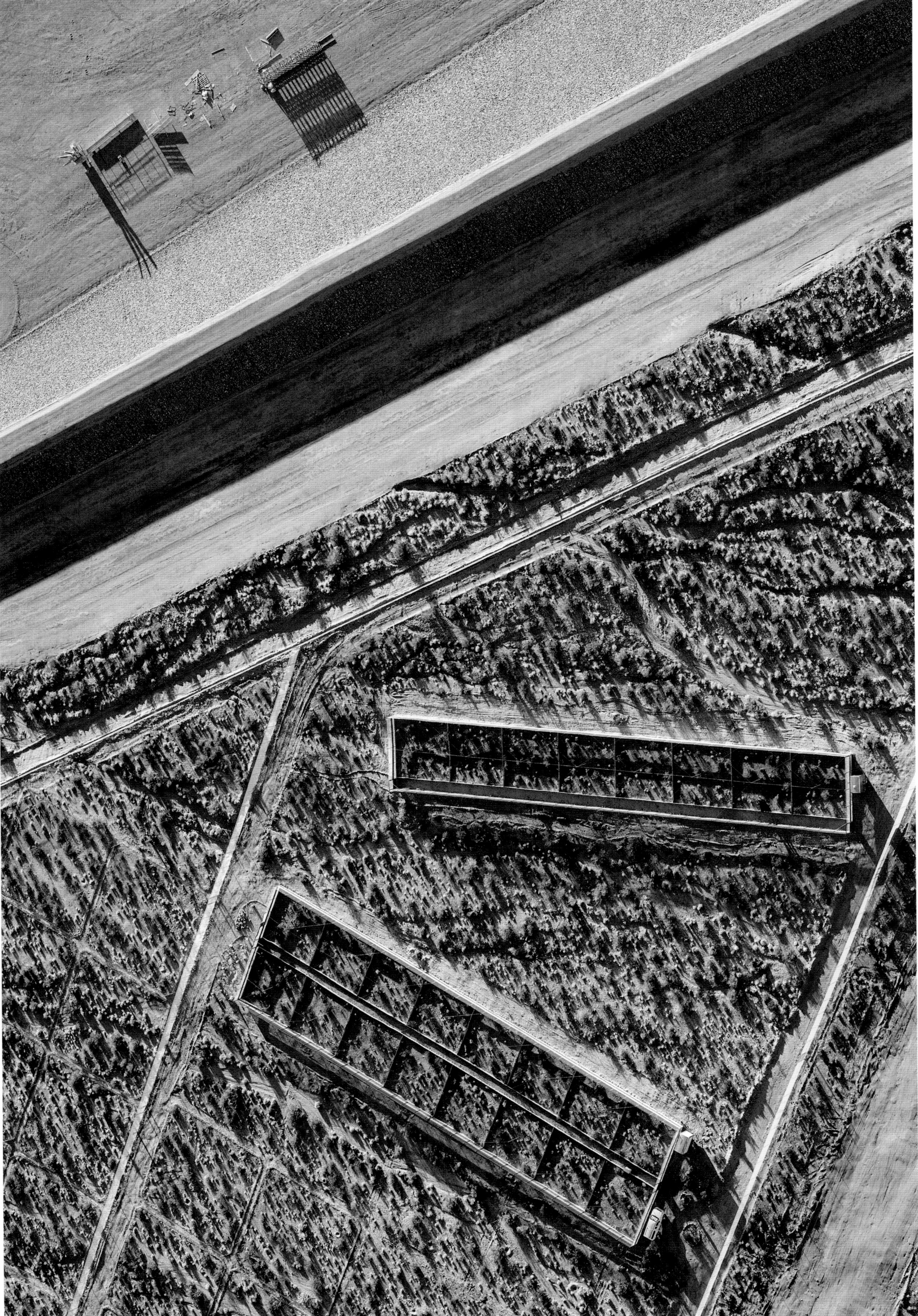

#9720, 21 MARCH 2013

IVANPAH SUBSTATION, OPERATIONS CENTER, AND JUVENILE TORTOISE NURSERY

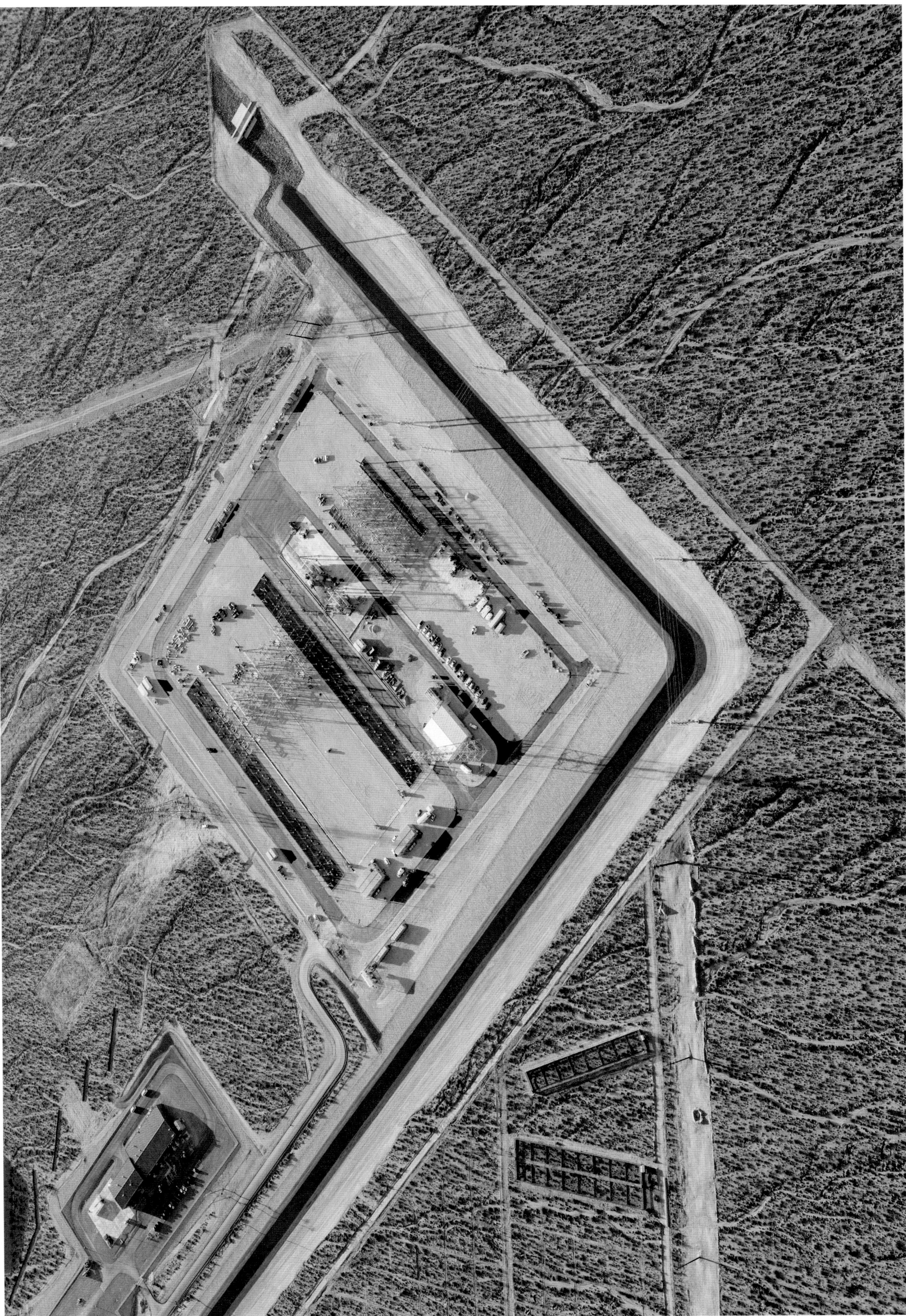

#11476, 5 SEPTEMBER 2013

HELIOSTATS AT NORTHERN BOUNDARY OF UNIT 3

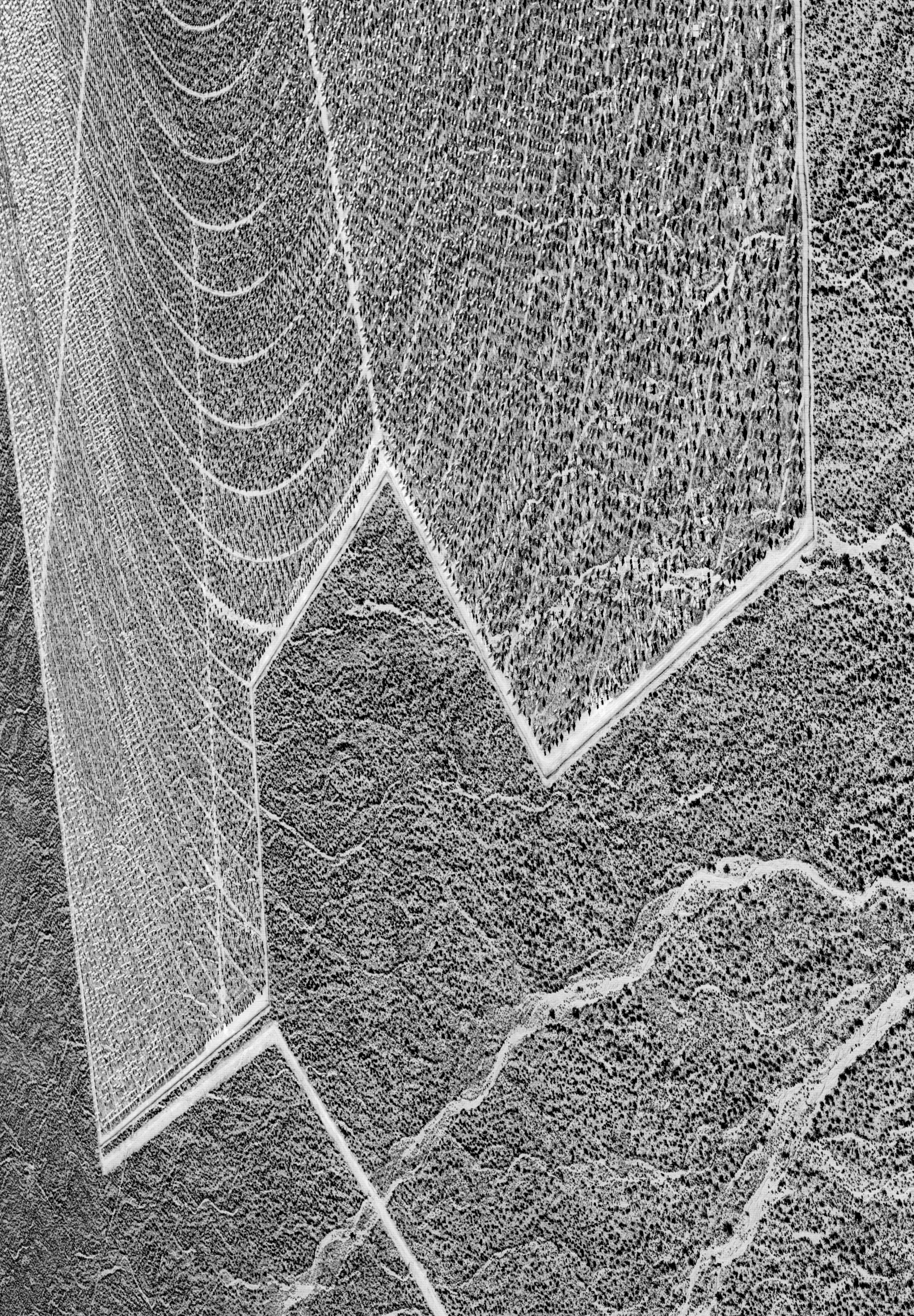

#10888, 25 JUNE 2013

VIEW NORTH OF IVANPAH AT DUSK

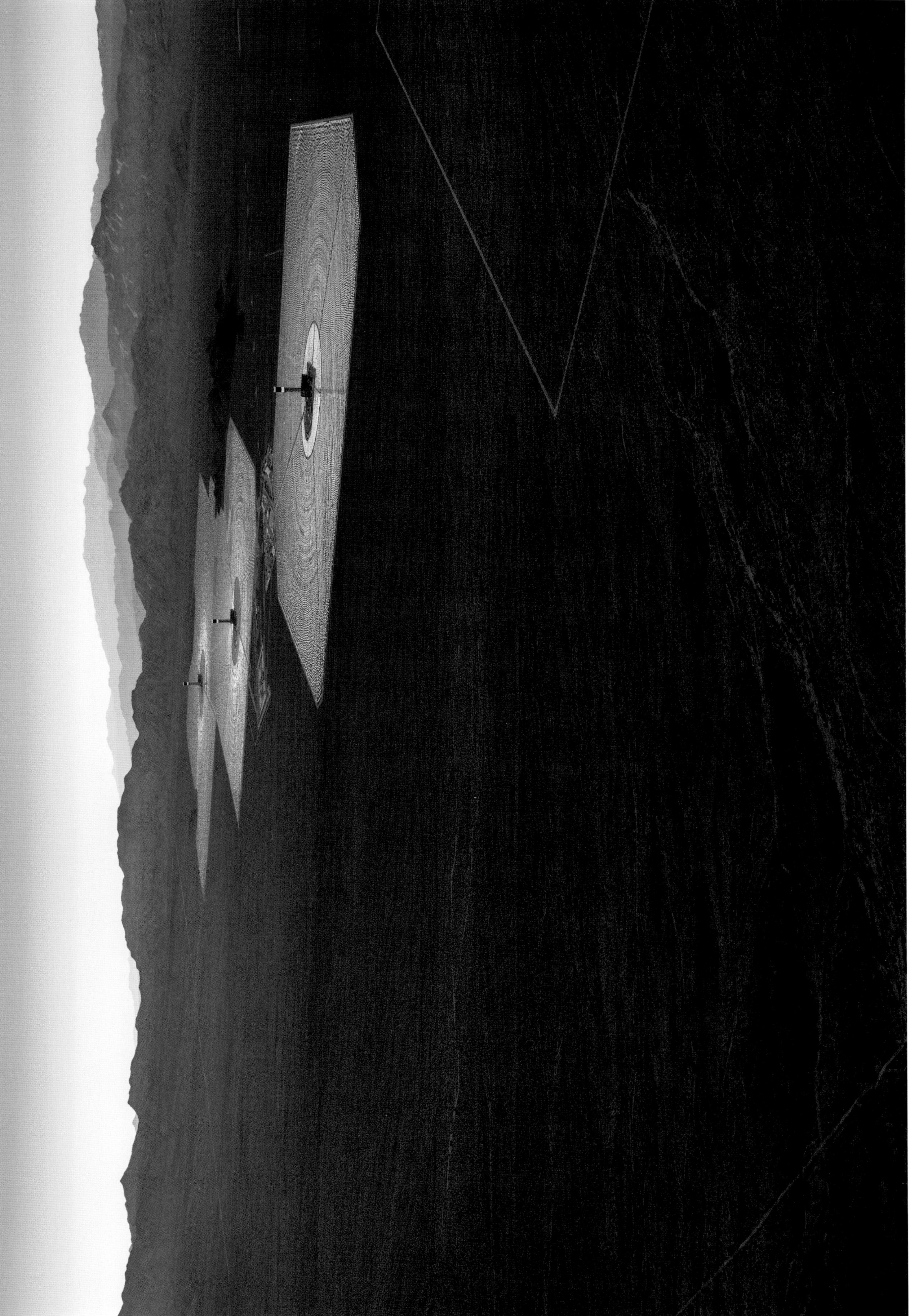

#10815, 25 JUNE 2013

VIEW NORTH OF UNIT 3 AT DUSK

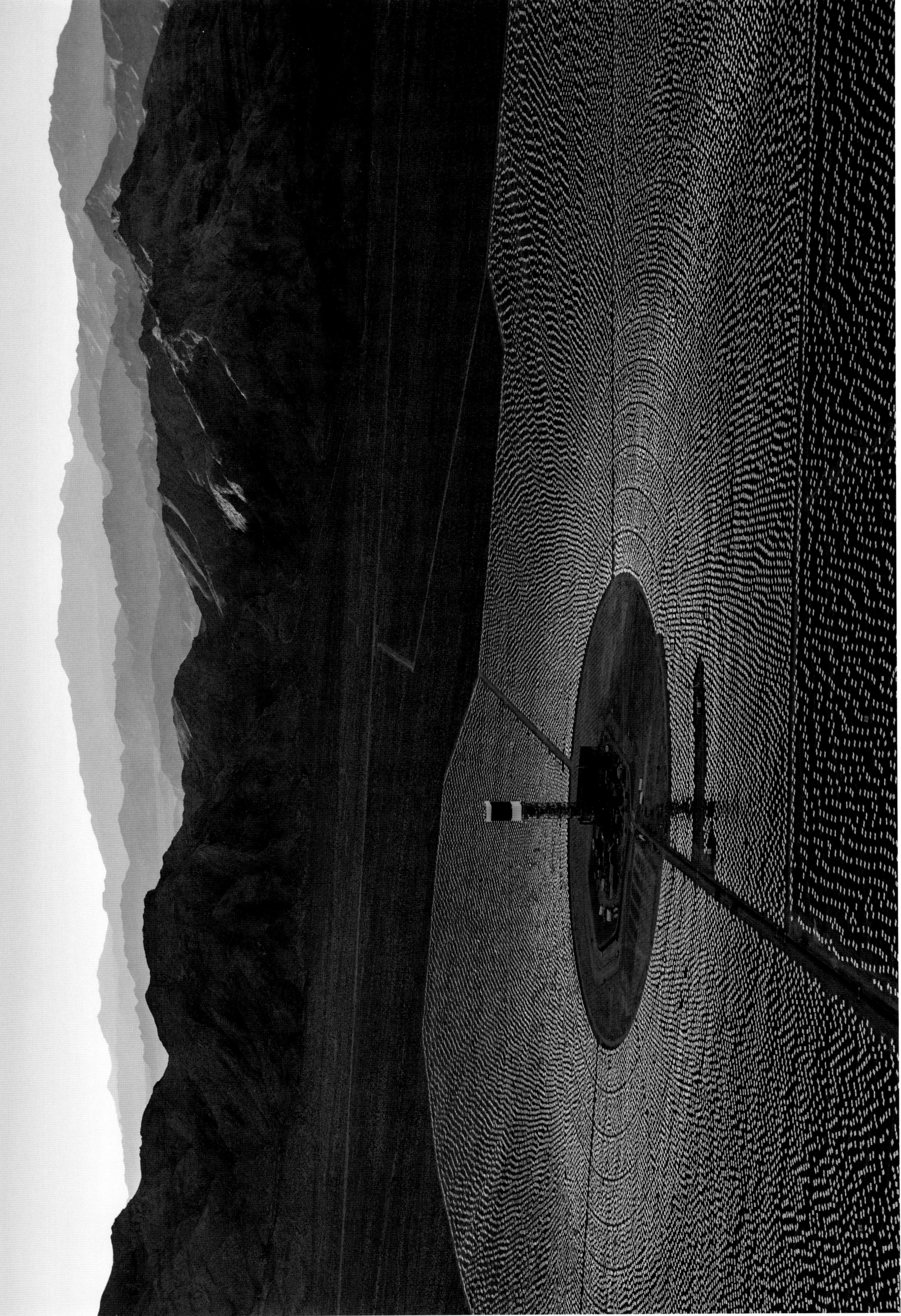

#11913, 1 OCTOBER 2013

VIEW NORTH FROM THE POWER TOWER OF UNIT 3 AT DUSK

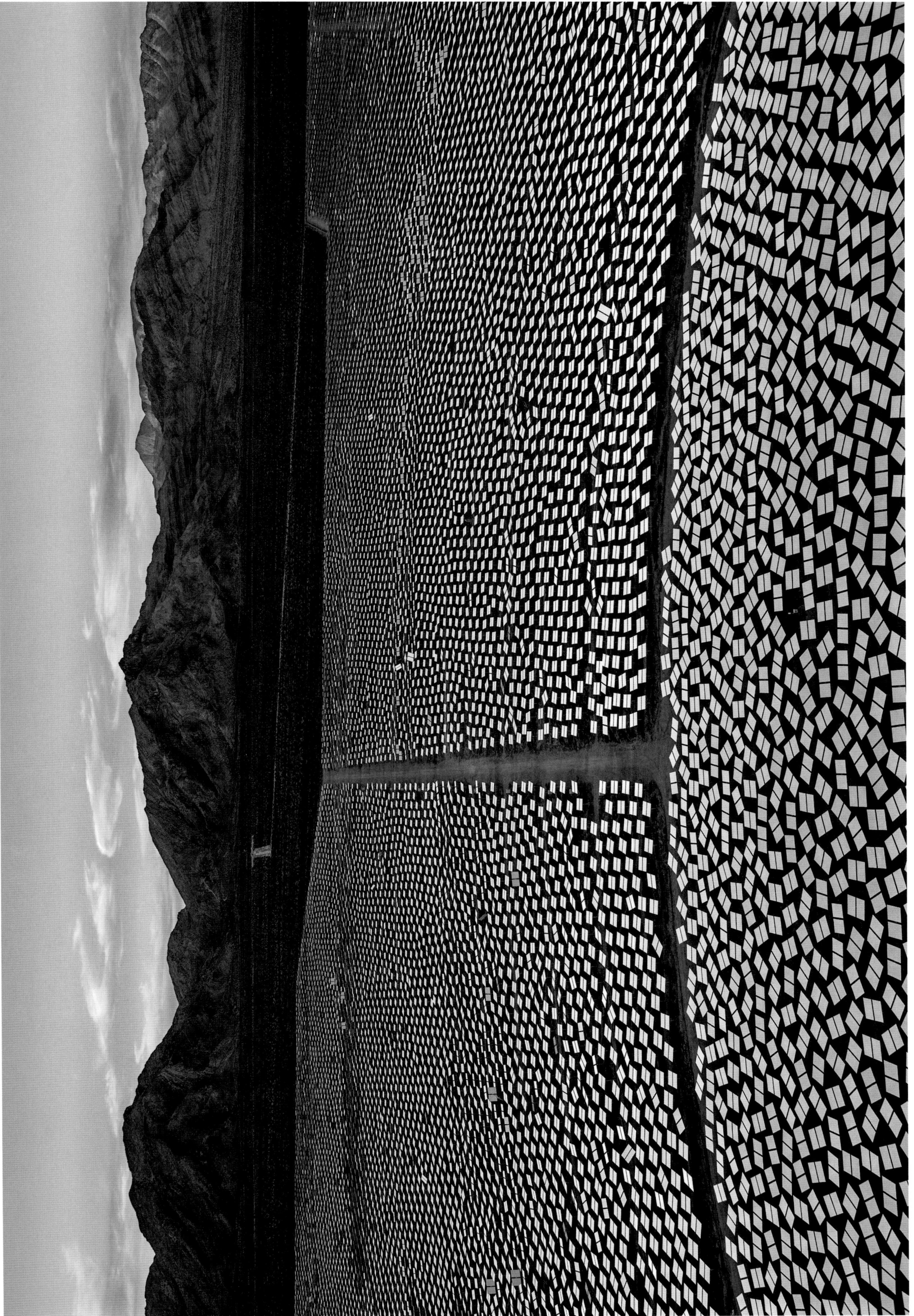

#10984, 4 SEPTEMBER 2013

FLUX TESTING, UNIT 3: HELIOSTATS CONCENTRATE THE SUN'S THERMAL ENERGY, SUPER-HEATING WATER TO CREATE STEAM, WHICH DRIVES A TURBINE TO GENERATE ELECTRICITY

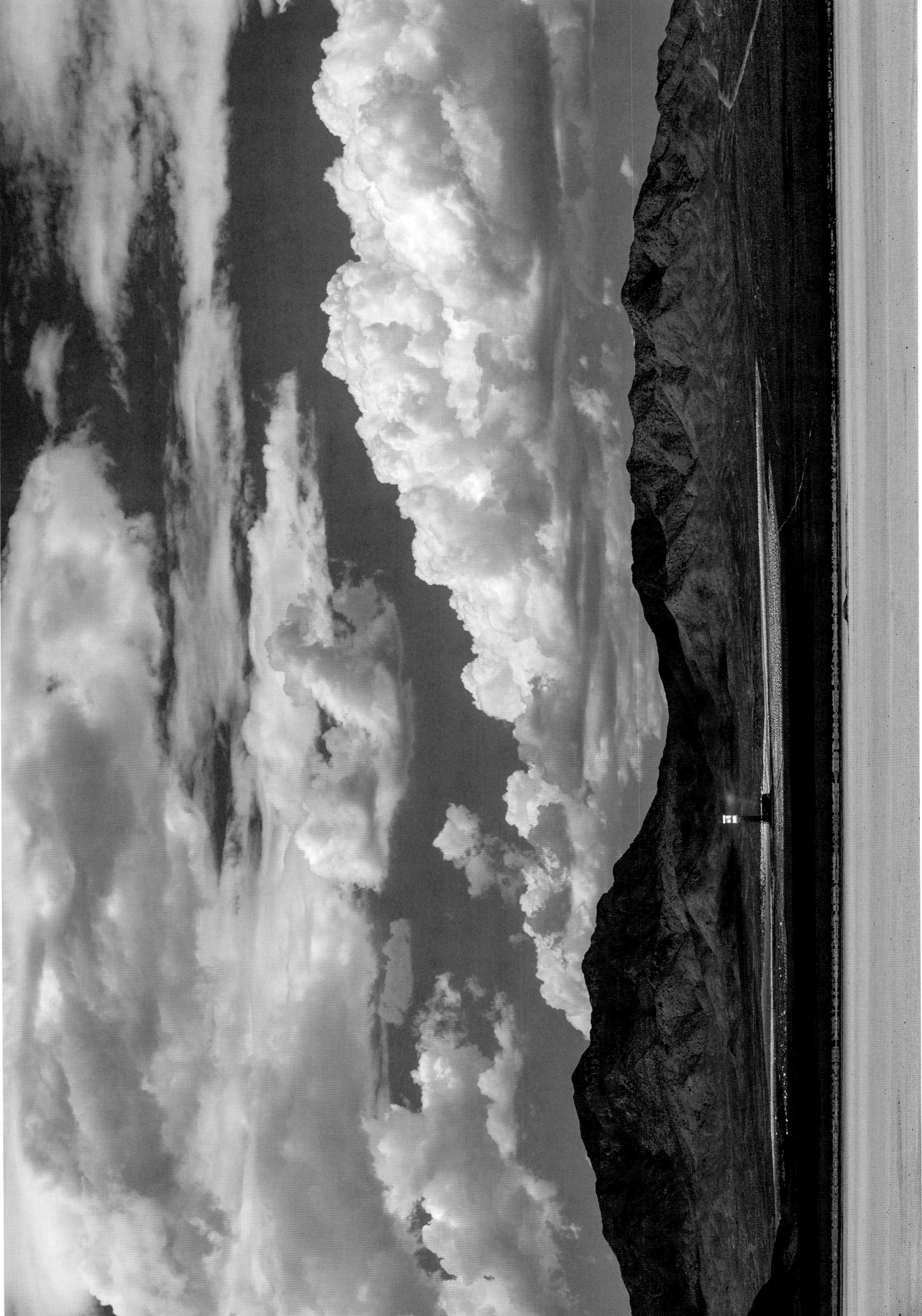

#11060, 4 SEPTEMBER 2013

VIEW NORTH OF UNITS 2 AND 3 WITH MOST HELIOSTATS IN HORIZONTAL (SAFE) MODE

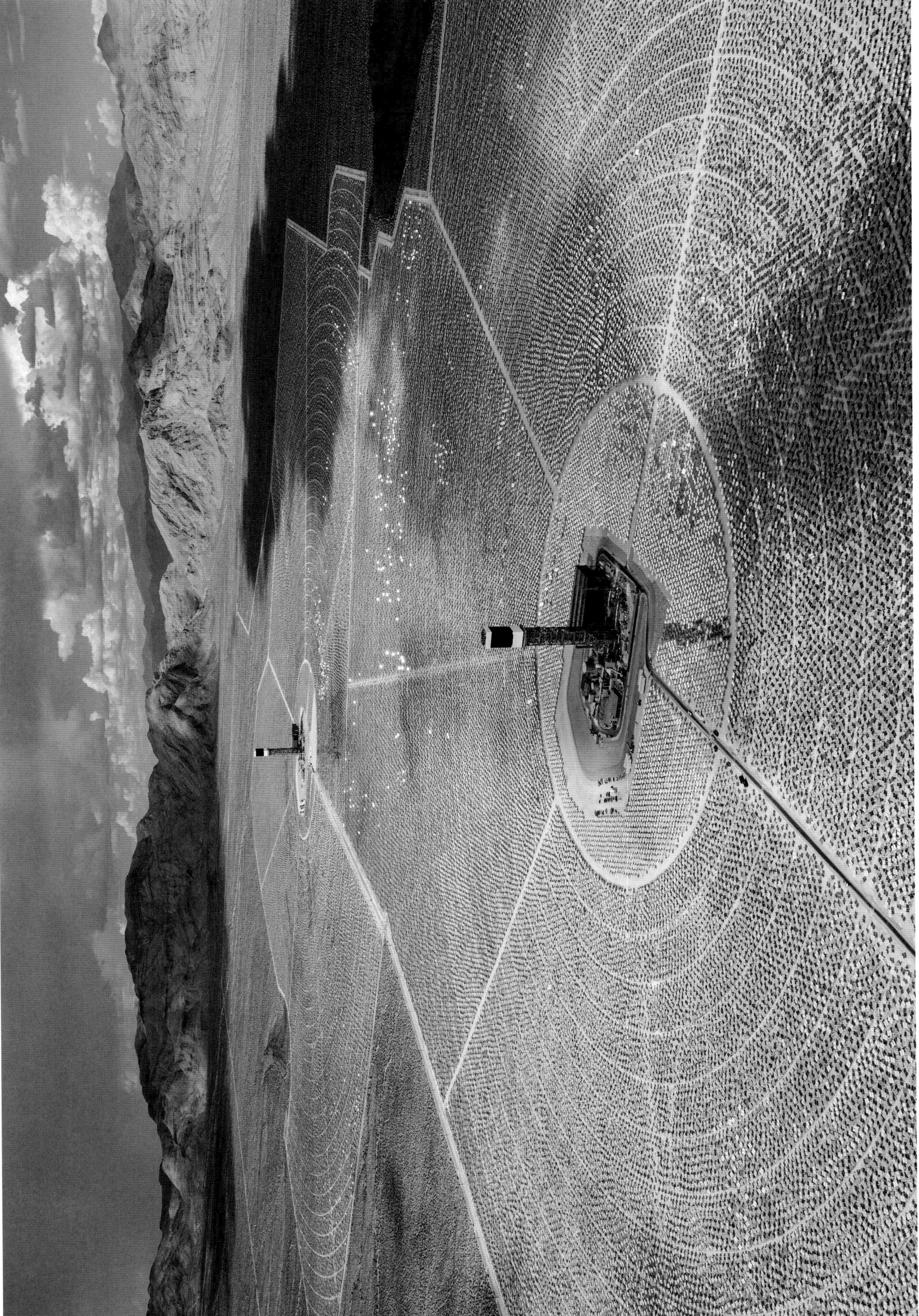

#11590, 5 SEPTEMBER 2013

FLUX TESTING, UNIT 3: HELIOSTATS CONCENTRATE THE SUN'S THERMAL ENERGY, SUPER-HEATING WATER TO CREATE STEAM, WHICH DRIVES A TURBINE TO GENERATE ELECTRICITY

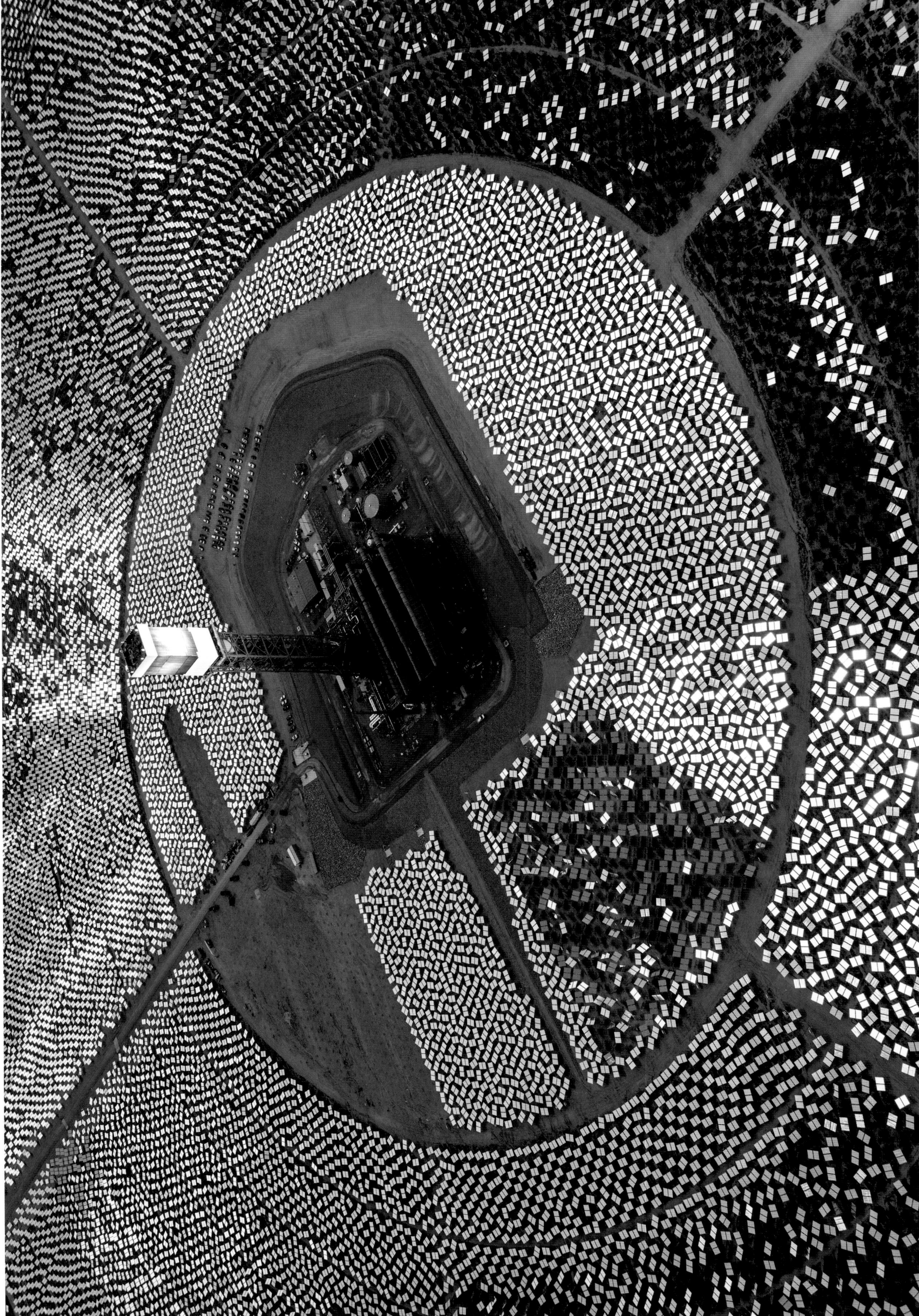

#16904, 24 SEPTEMBER 2014

HELIOSTATS FROM TOWER OF UNIT 2

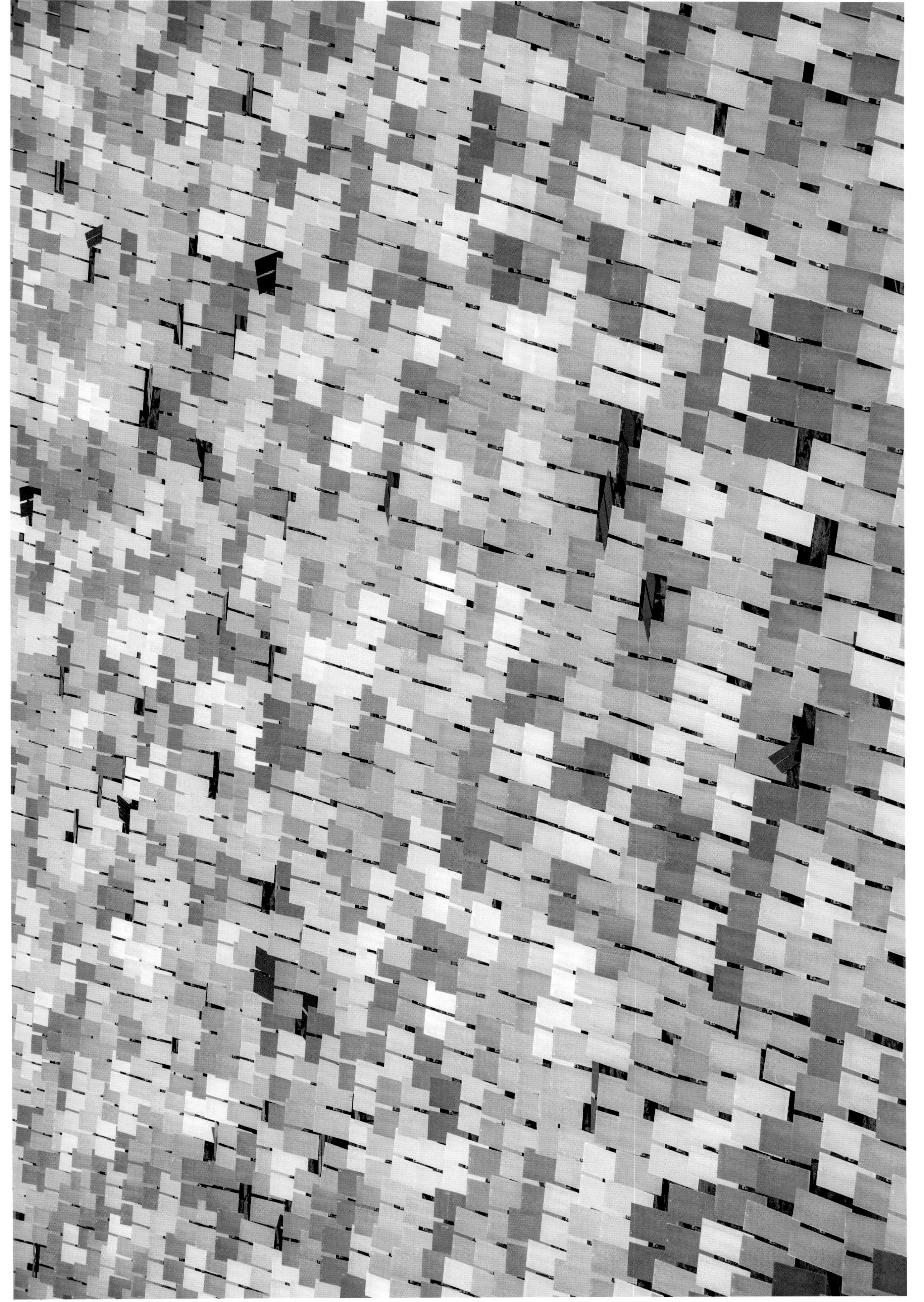

#11039, 4 SEPTEMBER 2013

VIEW WEST OF UNIT 2 AND CLARK MOUNTAIN

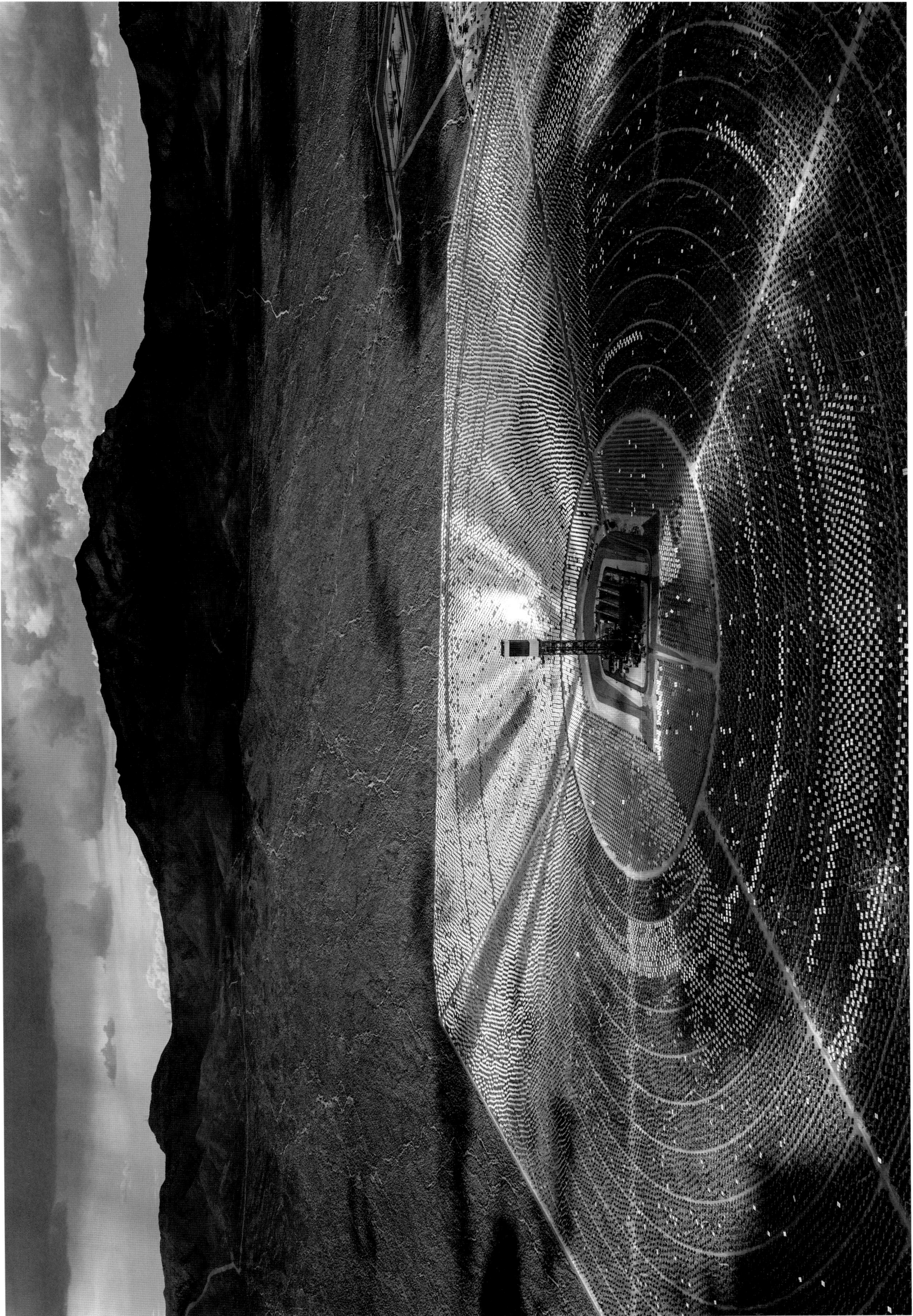

#14153, 3 FEBRUARY 2014

POWER PRODUCTION AT UNIT 2: ELECTRICAL POWER IS BEING DELIVERED TO THE GRID

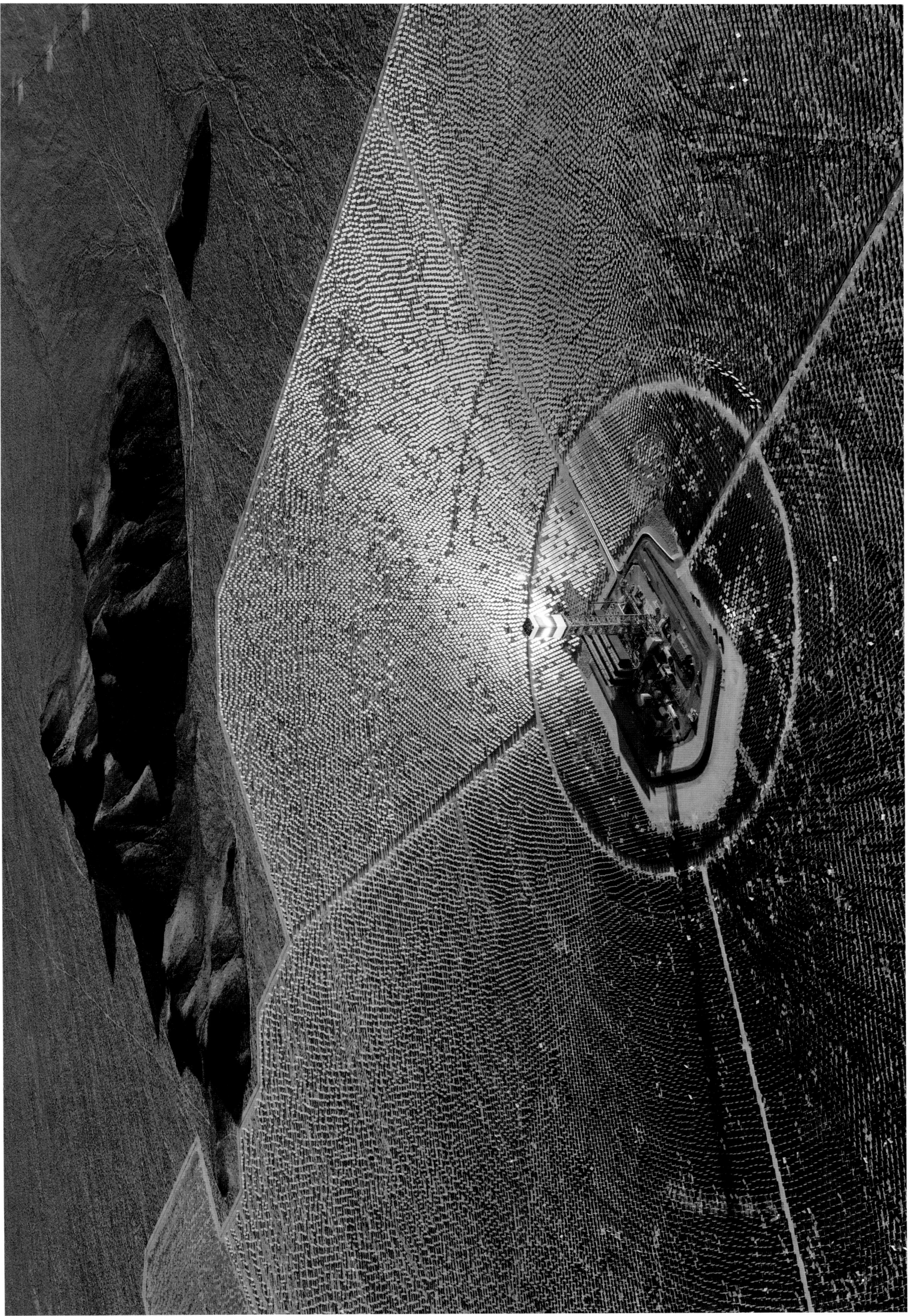

#14110, 3 FEBRUARY 2014

POWER PRODUCTION AT UNIT 1

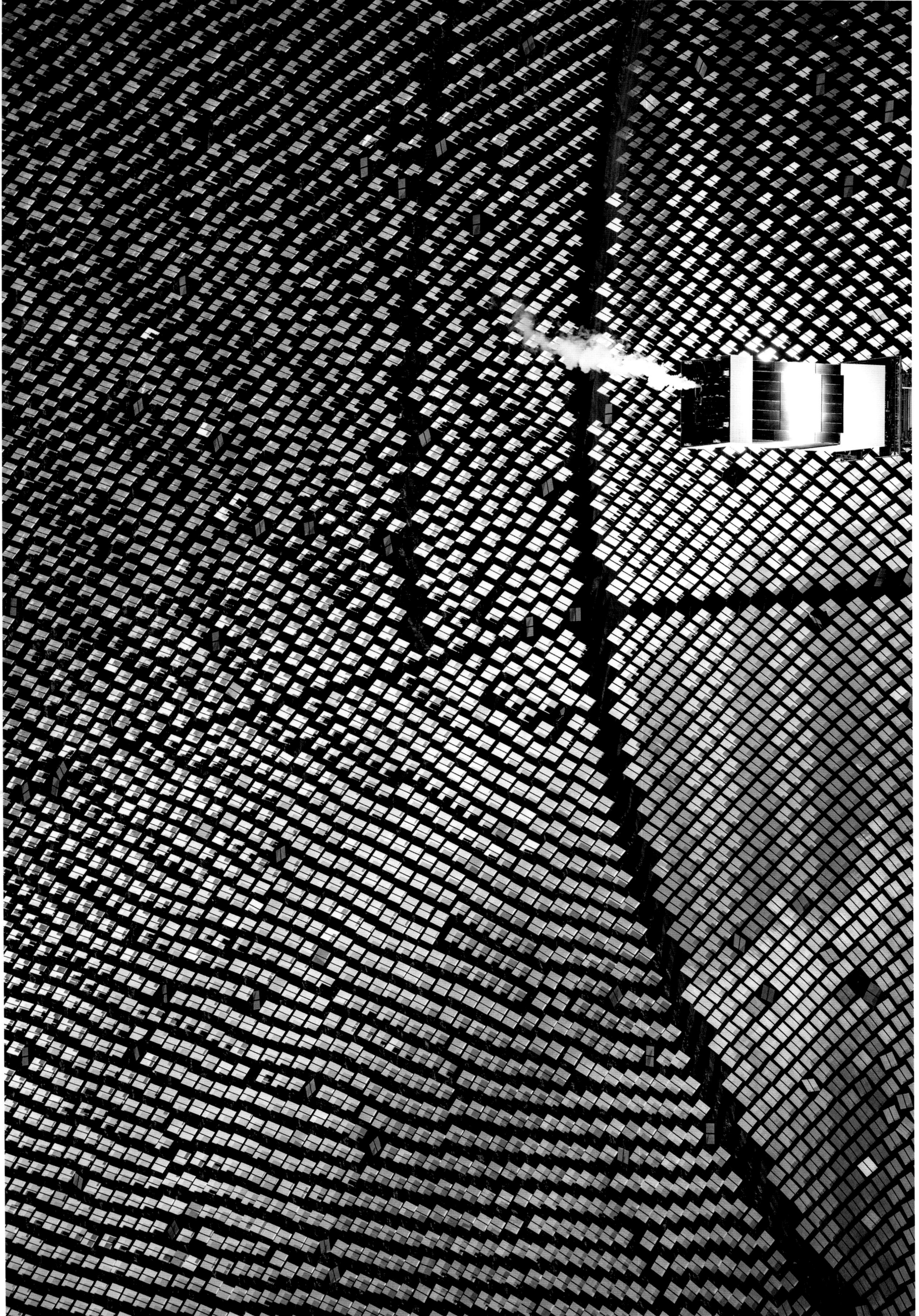

#13212, 1 NOVEMBER 2013

VIEW NORTH OF UNITS 1, 2, AND 3 AT DUSK

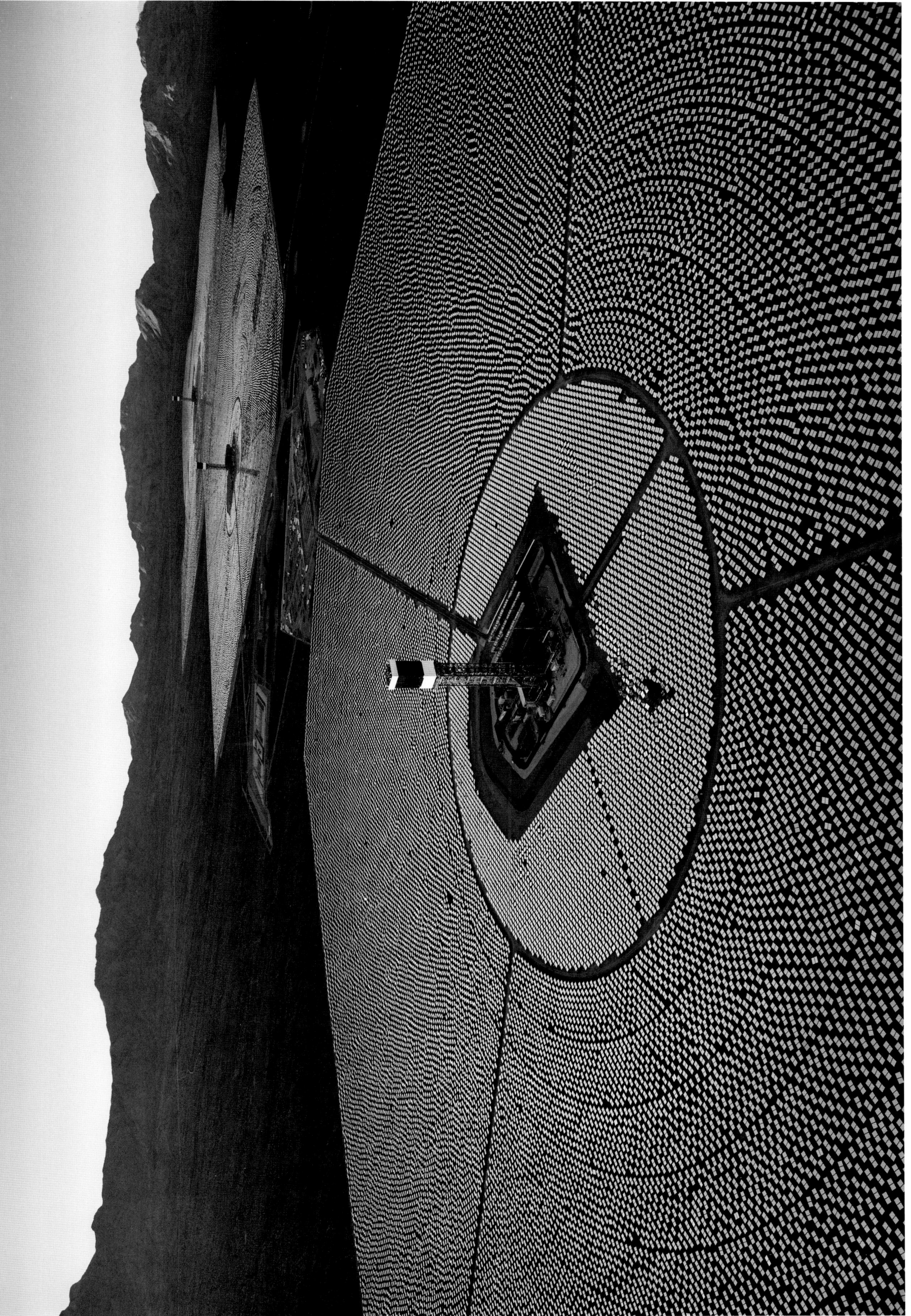

#14043, 3 FEBRUARY 2014

POWER PRODUCTION AT UNIT 2

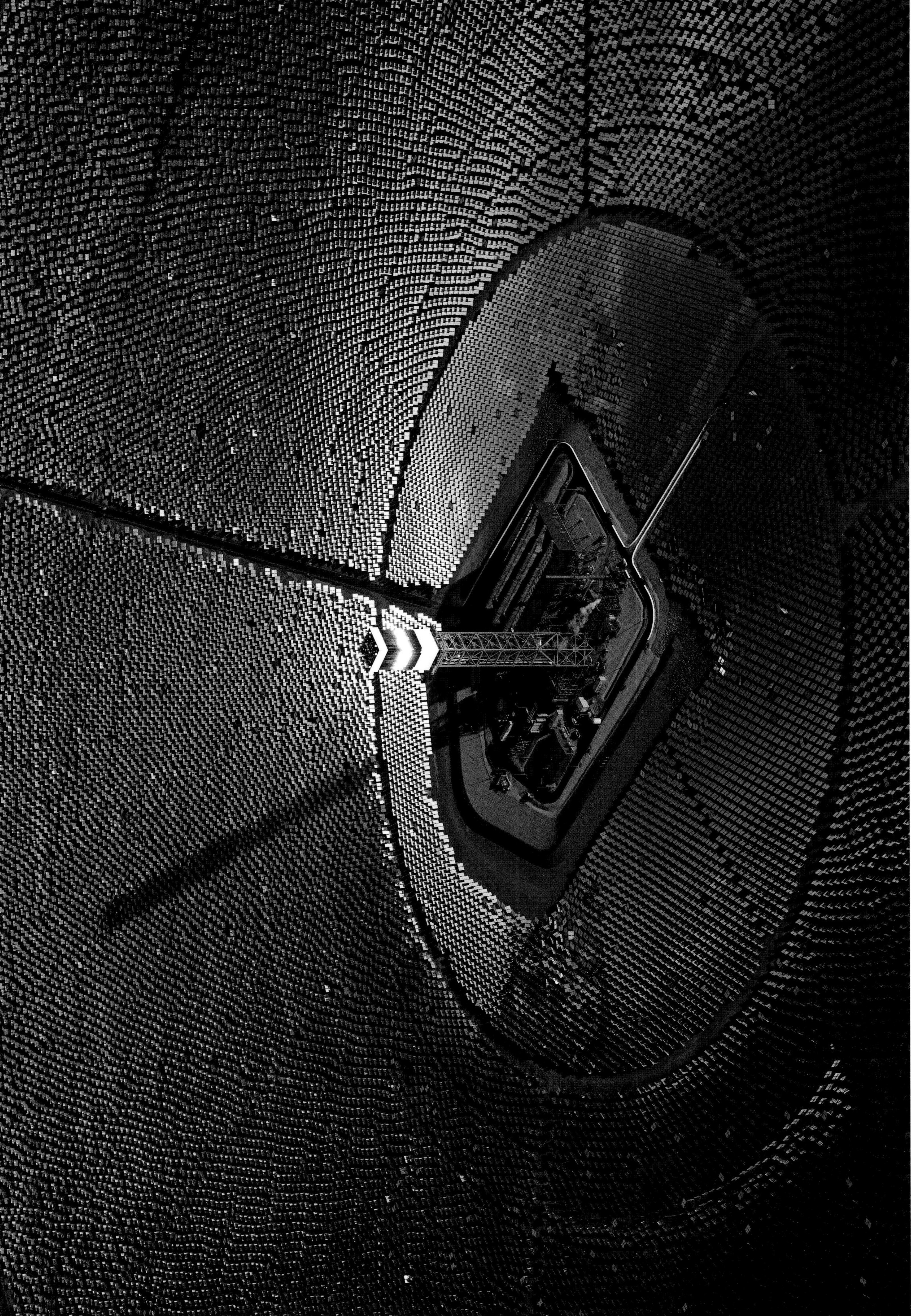

#17203, 24 SEPTEMBER 2014

POWER PRODUCTION AT UNIT 2

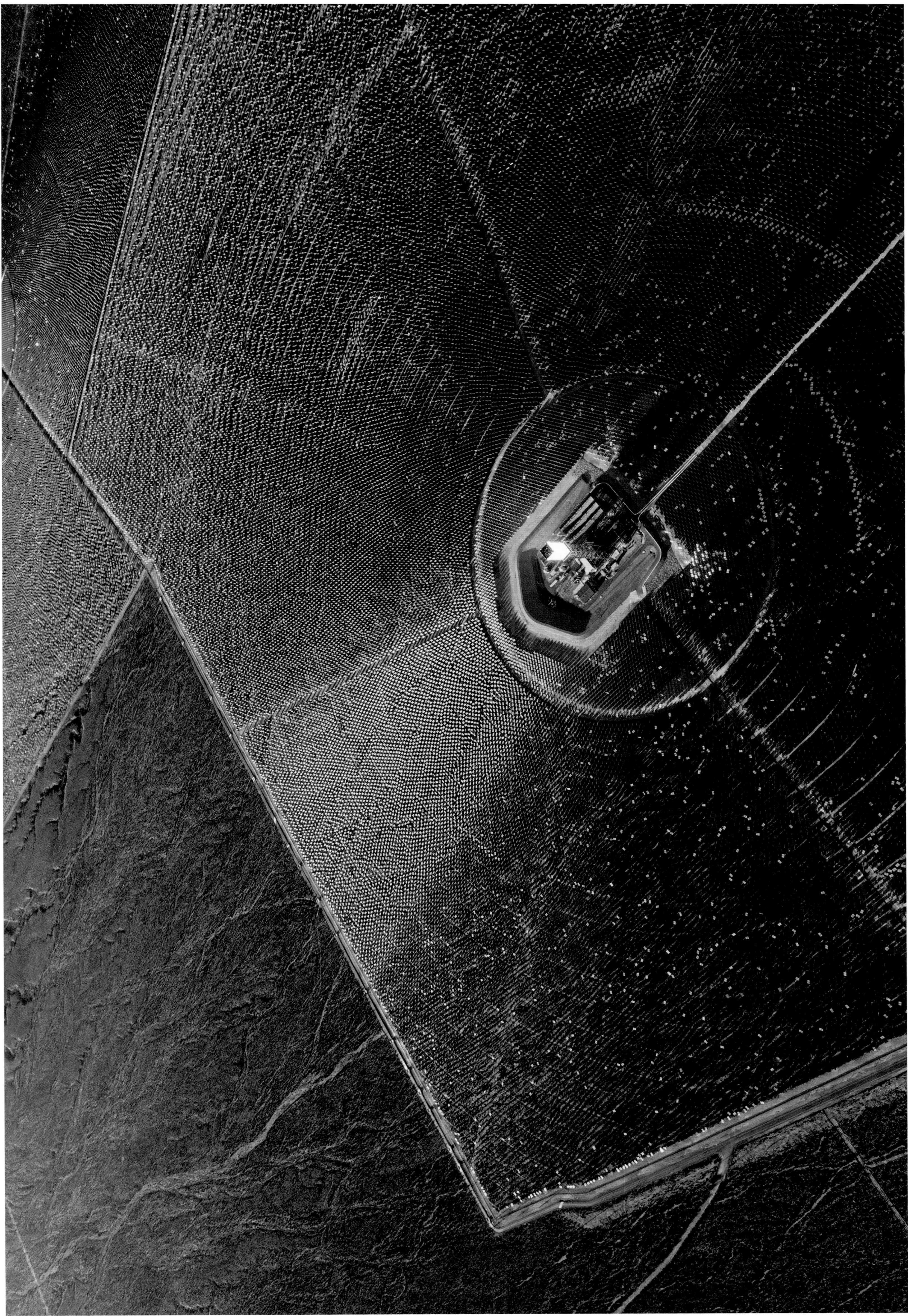

#14221, 3 FEBRUARY 2014

ALL THREE UNITS OF IVANPAH PRODUCING CONCENTRATED SOLAR POWER, VIEW TO THE SOUTHEAST

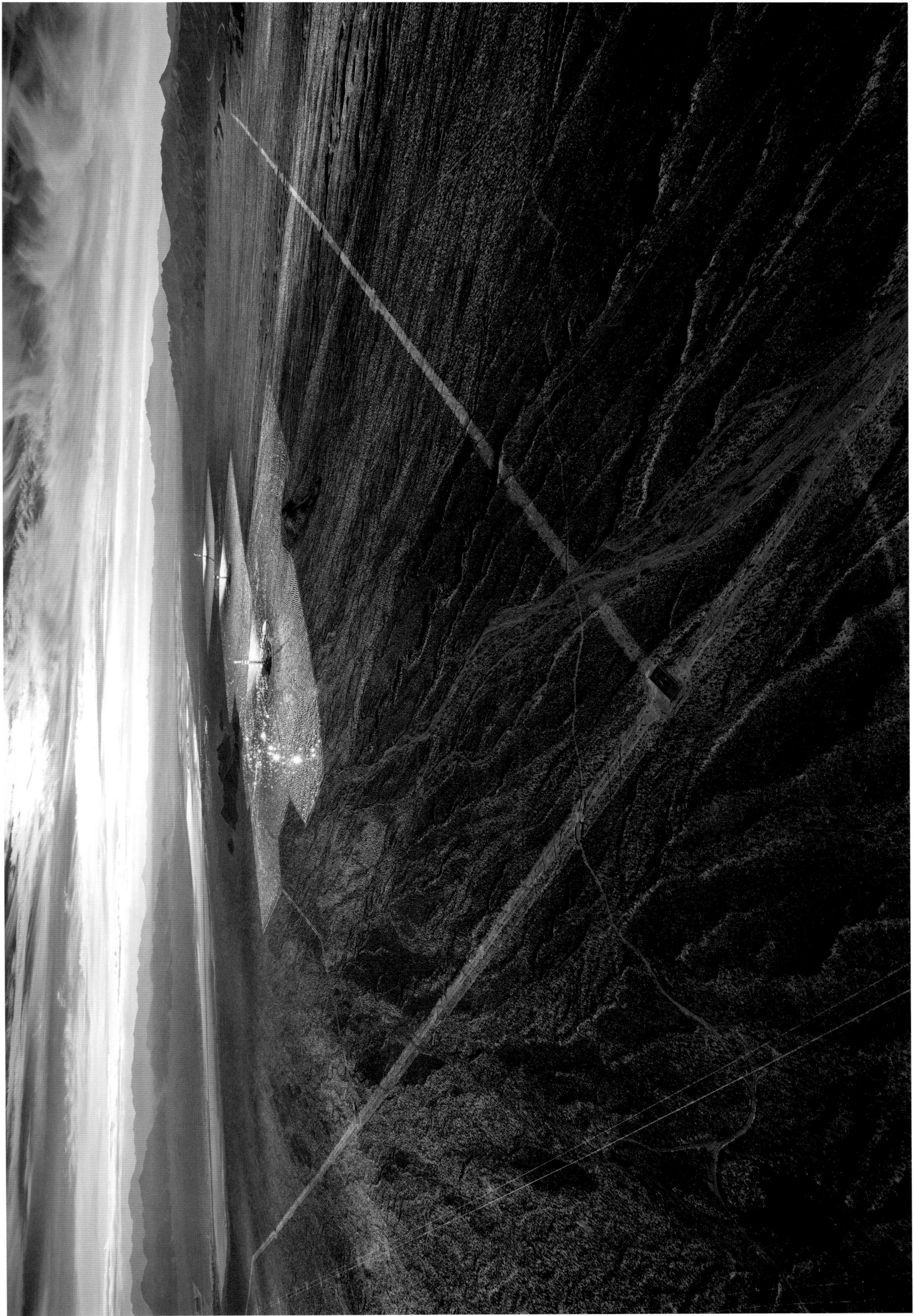

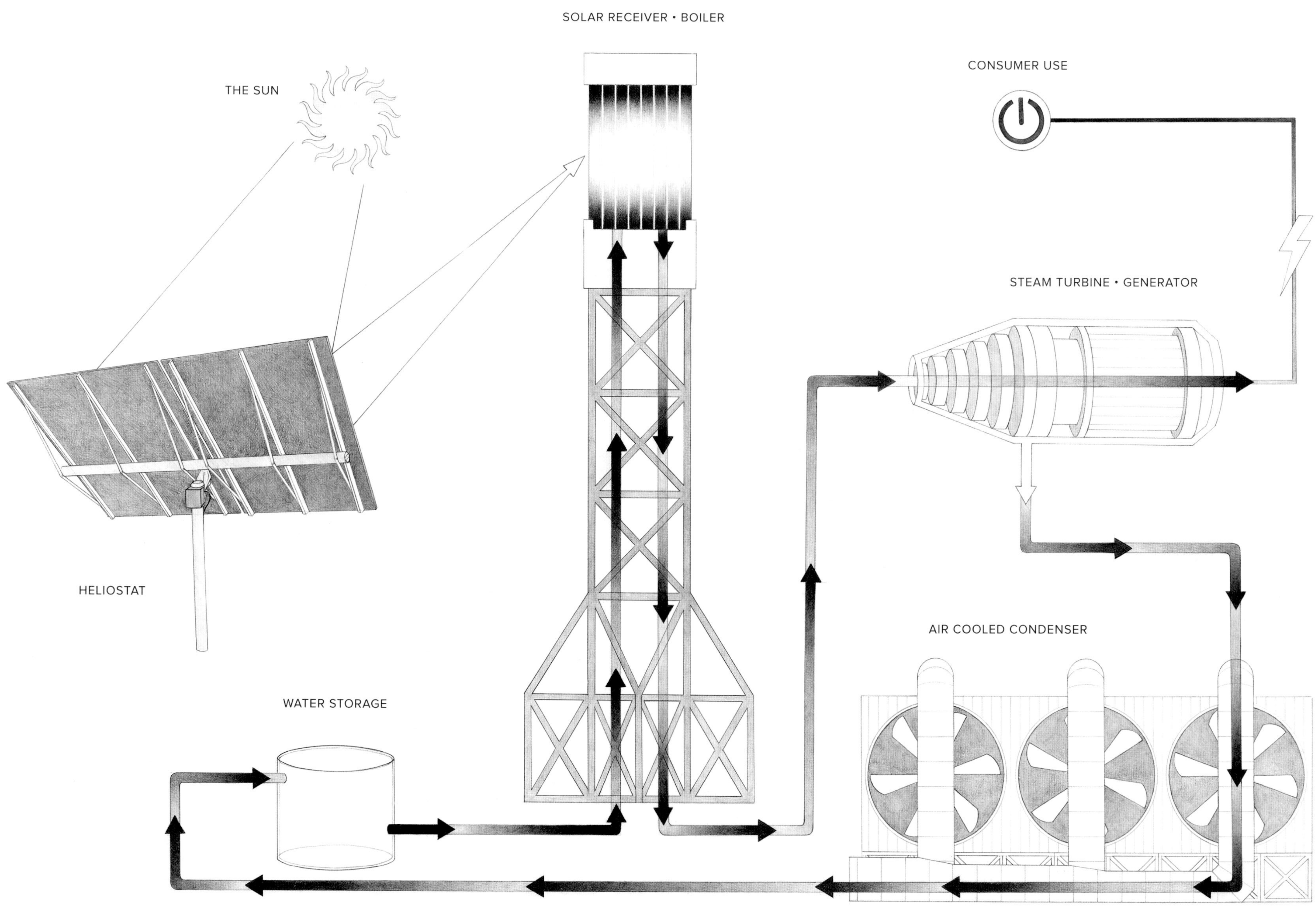

SOLAR RECEIVER • BOILER

THE SUN

CONSUMER USE

STEAM TURBINE • GENERATOR

HELIOSTAT

AIR COOLED CONDENSER

WATER STORAGE

IVANPAH SOLAR ELECTRIC GENERATING SYSTEM

Ivanpah Solar's concentrated solar thermal tower technology produces electricity the same way as fossil fuel power plants: by creating high-temperature steam to turn a conventional turbine. However, instead of using fossil fuels to create steam, it uses the sun's thermal energy.

Central to the technology is a solar-field design that utilizes thousands of heliostats, each consisting of two mirrors. Optimization software and a control system allow individual heliostats to track the sun in two dimensions, thereby reflecting sunlight to a boiler positioned atop a tower. When concentrated sunlight strikes the solar receiver, it heats water to create superheated steam, which is piped down from the boiler to a conventional steam turbine that generates electricity. Transmission lines carry the power to homes and businesses in southern California.

— Located on 14.2 square kilometers (about 5.5 square miles) of public land, managed by the US Bureau of Land Management

— Three-unit power tower system production: 377 megawatts (Net) / 392 megawatts (Gross) [Unit 1: 126 megawatts; Unit 2: 133 megawatts; Unit 3: 133 megawatts]

— Tower Height: 140 meters (459 feet)

— Number of Heliostats: 173,500 (2 mirrors per heliostat)

— Reflective Area per Heliostat: 15.2 square meters (a little over 163 square feet)

— Heliostat Solar-Field Aperture Area: 2,637,200 square meters (28,386,585 square feet; about 2.5 square kilometers or 1 square mile)

— Average Heliostat Installation Rate: 1 per minute during construction period

— Heliostat Placement Accuracy: +/- 10 centimeters (4 inches) of depth; 15 centimeters (6 inches) of leeway in location

— Boiler Type: Solar Receiver Steam Generator (SRSG)

— Cooling Method: Dry (air-cooled condenser)

— Water Consumption: 123,000 cubic meters per year (100 acre feet per year), equivalent to 300 homes per year

— Avoided Emissions: More than 400,000 metric tons of carbon dioxide (CO_2) each year

— Construction Jobs Created: More than 2,100 craft workers, a total of 2,636 workers at peak construction

— Owners: NRG Energy, Google, and BrightSource Energy

— EPC Contractor: Bechtel

— Customers: Pacific Gas & Electric; Southern California Edison

— Construction Commenced: October 2010

— Operational: December 2013

— Average Homes Served Annually: 140,000

FOREWORD

Robert Redford

When I first encountered Jamey Stillings' photographs of Ivanpah Solar in the Mojave Desert, I was captivated not only by their stark beauty, but by the questions his work raises in our quest to balance the growing demands of a consumer-based culture with the need to preserve Earth's natural spaces and resources. As the impacts of global climate change become clear, we must grasp that the sum of our human activities is having a huge and negative impact on this planet. Since the dawn of the Industrial Revolution, we have drilled, mined, and transformed much of Earth's wilderness, while burning enough coal, oil, and gas to radically raise the temperature of the atmosphere and oceans—a process that threatens to disrupt life, as we know it, by the end of the century. We face the urgent need to shift away from fossil fuels to energy sources that can profoundly reduce our greenhouse gas emissions.

Renewable energy is an essential part of our move toward a sustainable future. Yet, the challenging decisions we must make for its development are neither simple, nor clear. They require working through difficult sets of nuanced choices that force us to confront larger and sometimes contradictory issues about our priorities and the preservation or utilization of land and natural resources. Large utility-scale energy projects, in particular, must be weighed within the context of our continued fossil fuel dependence, while balancing local impacts with the Big Picture. Ivanpah Solar is symbolic of the challenges we face in assessing such issues.

Before construction commenced on the alluvial slopes between Interstate Highway 15 and Clark Mountain, fourteen square kilometers of public land were still part of the natural world—home to many species of flora and fauna, including the desert tortoise, listed as "threatened" under the Federal Endangered Species Act. To mitigate this issue, Ivanpah Solar's owners have spent millions of dollars to study and relocate the tortoises.

Now complete, the solar plant has become part of our growing human-altered landscape. At first blush, this shift seems antithetical to environmental efforts to limit our impact on the land. However, the trade-offs associated with this solar plant are more complex. All energy projects impact birds. Ivanpah Solar is no exception. But context and perspective are everything. A recent study estimates that bird deaths per gigawatt hour of electricity are seventeen times higher for fossil fuels, than for wind power, and, while comprehensive statistics are not yet available for concentrated solar, initial data is closer to wind than to fossil fuels.

Compared with electricity from natural gas and coal, Ivanpah reduces carbon dioxide emissions by 400,000 and 850,000 tons per year, respectively. How, then, do we weigh the positive impact on global flora and fauna of reducing our carbon footprint by ten to twenty-one billion tons over a period of twenty-five years?

As a long-time environmental activist and supporter of the arts, I find Jamey's work compelling for its ability to observe and respect both nature and human-made environments, while drawing us to the dynamic energy and tension created at their intersections. Storytellers have the power to broaden our minds and shift the way we think about complex environmental issues. Through his continued documentation of renewable energy development, Jamey enters into the cast of characters shaping the way we navigate our energy future.

INTRODUCTION

Anne Wilkes Tucker

In recent years, Jamey Stillings' career as a commercial photographer has shifted emphasis from briefer engagements to long-term personal projects. Since 2009, his primary undertakings feature the construction of massive structures: the Mike O'Callaghan-Pat Tillman Memorial Bridge, a 581 meter (1905 foot) bridge soaring over the Colorado River downstream from Hoover Dam, and Ivanpah Solar, the 392-megawatt concentrated solar power plant that now stretches over more than fourteen square kilometers (about five square miles) of the Mojave Desert. His analytical mind was fascinated and challenged by the skills and systems required to realize these ventures, but the artist in him loved their brut physical glory and complicated visual and physical relationships to the environments that they came to dominate.

His goal was to document each project to its completion. To track their progress required adjusting his schedule to cover each stage, mastering new technical skills, and most critically, preconceiving pictures that would graphically convey his impressions of the projects and the sites. The pictures are detailed, but mere description was not his aim. For instance, the dramatic sight of a half-built bridge ending in midair over a chasm seems more remarkable and unnerving when seen at night. Sunlight solidifies the stone and steel forms that were conversely less substantial in the gloaming. The site's lights at night add a touch of wonderland.

To document Ivanpah, Stillings shot aerial images, first of the contractor's rings etched into the earth, and then of the placement of thousands of heliostats (mirrors) along the etched lines until they nearly obscure the land. The three giant towers, each placed at the center of a solar field to catch the mirrors' reflected rays of light, compete in scale with the surrounding mountains. One journalist described the towers as a "clean-tech version of *The Lord of the Rings*."[1] However clever, this "tinged with evil" implication opposes Stillings' belief in the importance of the project. Although he is well informed about aspects that can be deservedly criticized, such as the dangers to birds[2] and disruption of the natural landscape, he is convinced that the public gain outweighs objections, and his works embody that optimism.

Stillings' title for the series, *Changing Perspectives*, of which *The Evolution of Ivanpah Solar* is the first chapter, has a double meaning. First, it works on a descriptive level: he traced the changes at the site from before construction commenced through completion. "On one hand," he wrote, "I am looking from the air at a specific landscape in the Mojave that has changed radically over three years with construction, time of year, and the specifics of each day. Every visit required me to look freshly (and quickly) at the land, then work intuitively to interpret what I saw."[3] For instance, he had only fifteen to thirty minutes each morning to work with the optimal oblique light of the sun, and he needed early-morning or late-afternoon light for the long shadows that helped delineate the mirrors from the ground, as well as the natural erosion lines in the earth. The title's other level of meaning is aspirational, conveying his hope that beyond their aesthetic appeal, the pictures will lead to questions and interests that transform viewers' understanding about the nature of solar energy and its potential to encourage "more careful choices about use of the Earth's land and resources."

When asked about his photographic influences, Stillings has cited *Life* magazine's Margaret Bourke-White for her sense of composition and use of abstraction, and Lewis Hine for his powerful photographic series on the building of the Empire State Building.[4] Both of these photographers worked in the first-half of the twentieth century and shared Stillings' belief in photography's potential to influence thought; they also shared a celebratory approach to industrial progress, although previously Hine had campaigned against industry's uncontrolled abuses of child labor. Bourke-White was a pioneer of industrial photography who worked first for *Fortune* magazine, and then secured the cover story for the inaugural issue of *Life* magazine (1936) with a dramatic image of Fort Peck Dam in Montana. In classic Bourke-White style, she found the structure's rhythm in a receding view of its towers. Lewis Hine was 56 years old when he received a commission to photograph the construction of the Empire State Building. Hine photographed the site from the time of its excavation in January 1930 to the building's topping in April 1931, working from increasing heights as the structure grew to 103 stories. In the process, he took many of the same risks as the workers, who were his central focus. More like Bourke-White than Hine, Stillings includes the workers, but they serve as reminders that these are man-built structures that dwarf their makers. Hine's laborers appear skilled, heroic, and at times, endearingly human. The biggest shift represented in Stillings' work from the optimistic industrial pictures of the 1920s and 1930s is the creation of energy from renewable sources, and the process's dependency on digital technology for the operation of each mirror's position relative to the sun and the towers. Despite their scale, these solar installations have a delicacy, whereas the generation of power in the 1920s was conveyed through views such as those of molten steel pouring from giant vats or of black smoke pouring from smoke stacks, which, in the Depression of the 1930s, was a sign of employment, not pollution.

The thread that binds the "Bridge" and "Ivanpah" projects is Stillings' utilization of patterns and geometric relationships that are both inherent in mechanical designs and heightened by his various approaches. For instance, some repeated configurations exist on the simplest level in two different pictures of the "Bridge" project. In one image, the bridge's arch is mirrored by its shadow; in another, the semicircular lip of the dam is echoed by the bridge's supporting arch. However, in the "Ivanpah" work, the patterns are more complex and massive in scale. At the earliest stages, the floor plan of the project methodically slices across the Mojave's undulating and crisscrossing ridges. Eventually, these etched lines are obscured by the seemingly endless circles of 347,000 mirrors that are each about the size of a garage door.[5] Stillings has described the project as Wagnerian in scale—a scale at which abstraction moves toward metaphor. Picture-by-picture the desert's transformation is preserved; also recorded is his shifting between descriptive documentation of mechanisms, men, process, and context to lyrical abstraction on a majestic scale. Both approaches, Stillings has said, lead viewers to ponder "our individual and collective relationship to the world."[6]

Our regard for machines and their relevance to our future is intimately tied to photography's history. Machines and tools have been popular subjects since the mid-19th century for reasons as simple as the pleasure in formal elegance derived from their metal surfaces and clean designs, and as complex as their embodiment of our desires or fears for the future, either as symbols of power and progress, or as unwelcome invasions. The solar fields of Ivanpah are a next step in the evolution that includes reactions ranging from fascination to horror. The Eiffel tower, assembly lines, speeding trains, planes, and rockets are samplings of historic inventions that became symbols of their eras, but not without resistance from detractors. Spectacular photographs have preserved this march to modernity and beyond. Ivanpah Solar is a historic marker of our era, bringing major technologies and cultural changes, and preserved in Stillings' timely, graphic, and memorable photographs.

NOTES

1. Diane Cardwell and Matthew L Wald, "A Huge Solar Plant Opens, Facing Doubts about Its Future," *New York Times*, February 14, 2014.
2. According to Stillings, more birds are killed by cats and by hitting buildings and homes or coal power installations than from hitting solar- or wind-generating energy plants.
3. Email to author February 1, 2014.
4. Ibid.
5. Stillings' views of the man-marked land visually reference ancient land art that is large-scale and mysterious because of its unknown origins or purpose, and can only be perceived fully from above, which was not possible when they were created. Stillings became aware of such ancient sites while in graduate school at the Rochester Institute of Technology (1979–1981) with Marilyn Bridges, whose first major photographic series was aerial recordings of the two-thousand-year-old Nazca Lines in Peru.
6. Email to the author July 14, 2014.

REFLECTIONS ON THE MOJAVE SUN

Bruce Barcott

In the cool of the desert night, Jamey Stillings and I roll out of Las Vegas into the dark Mojave Desert. It's a little past four in the morning. With the glitz of the Strip in our rearview, we follow Interstate 15 south across dry desert lakes and wide alluvial fans, through miles of scrub and sand. The road is lonely, just a few long-haul truckers and crapped-out gamblers limping home to Los Angeles. It's a quiet time for humans, but out there beyond the asphalt there's action in the desert. Owls and coyotes are hunting. Bats are darting after moths. Cacti and creosote open their pores to drink in the air's moisture. Now and then a sign marks a lonely outpost: Sloan, Jean, Primm, once-hopeful townsites that never matured into towns. About eight kilometers past Primm, on the California side of the border, we turn onto a road leading into the faint outline of the Clark Mountains. Our headlights catch a sign: Ivanpah Solar Project.

As I write, Ivanpah stands as the largest concentrated solar power installation in the world. It's also one of the most controversial. The $2.2 billion project, commissioned in January 2014, is capable of producing 392 megawatts, enough electricity to power 140,000 homes during peak demand. Like a lot of megaprojects, it took a consortium of major players to make Ivanpah happen. BrightSource Energy designed it. The American people, under the auspices of the US Bureau of Land Management, let out the public land for lease. Ivanpah's owners—NRG (50%), Google (30%), and BrightSource (20%)—financed and own the project with help from a federal government loan guarantee. Bechtel built it. NRG operates it. PG&E and Southern California Edison purchase its power under 25-year contracts. Everything about the project is big.

It's so dark that I can't make out where we are. We're among the heliostats before I realize it. Heliostats are the 173,500 pairs of mirrors that reflect the sun onto Ivanpah's three power towers. Each tower is 140 meters (459 feet) tall, four-fifths the height of the Washington Monument. The mirrors stand upright at night in what their keepers call "sleep position," so when you drive among them in the pre-dawn gloaming it's tough to make them out, what with the hall of mirrors effect and all. Dark reflecting dark reflecting dark...

"It's like an immense art installation," I say to Jamey.

He nods.

Jamey's been documenting the creation of Ivanpah for years, so these mirror-made mirages are nothing new to him. But coming upon them with fresh eyes, my mind can't help but think of the monoliths of Easter Island, and the light-and-sensory artwork of James Turrell. I can't wait to see what happens when the sun comes up.

We pass through security and find our way to NRG's control room, a spacious chamber with computer consoles, dozens of flat screen monitors, and about ten control room engineers. It's 4:46 in the morning. We're here just in time to see the night crew fire up the auxiliary boilers.

The "aux boilers," as the engineers call them, are fueled by natural gas. If the night crew times it right, the aux boilers help the main boilers reach operating pressure just as the sun hits the mirrors. This pre-heating lets the engineers maximize Ivanpah's solar output, sending renewable power to the grid immediately, instead of using the first hour of sunshine to prime the system.

At 5:45 in the morning, the night crew hands over control to the day staff. They exchange notes.

"Unit 1?"

"Blowdowns are all reset. Ready to go."

Ivanpah is one complex made up of three distinct units. Each has one power tower surrounded by 50,000 to 60,000 heliostats.

"Unit 2?"

"Unit 2, we're ready, our boiler's coming up."

Unit 3 is down for maintenance but will come online later in the morning.

Dawn arrives. Out in the desert, nocturnal owls, rats, mice, and bats retreat to their burrows. They want nothing of the day's blasting heat. The heliostats, controlled by computers, slowly rotate into position. The first faint light shines on the dark band of the power towers.

At 8:02, Unit 1 comes online. It starts small, generating six megawatts. Then nine. Then eighteen. At 8:14, an engineer calls from across the room, "We're synched!"

Solar power shoots down the line. In San Francisco, customers of PG&E turn on their radios and heat up their coffee with Ivanpah energy. In Los Angeles, Southern California Edison brightens traffic lights and gives air conditioners their hum with power from the sun.

LIFE IN THE DESERT

The Mojave is a deceptive place. The driest and smallest of North America's four deserts—it's a bit smaller than Ireland—the Mojave encompasses an extreme range of topography and temperature. The gentle snow-capped peak of Mt. Charleston rises to 3,632 meters (11,916 feet), a mere 46 kilometers (28 miles) west of Las Vegas. It's part of the Mojave just as much as Death Valley, the lowest (86 meters, or 282 feet, below sea level) and hottest place in the United States. In outline, the Mojave is lumpy and misshapen, like a deerskin tossed over the meeting point of California, Nevada, and Arizona.

Its defining quality is the difficulty of sustaining life within it. Anyone who's round-tripped from Los Angeles to Las Vegas knows the Mojave as the journey's major crossing, a sandy sea that requires preparation, supplies, and good luck to reach the other side. "The Mojave is a big desert and a frightening one," John Steinbeck once wrote. "It's as though nature tested a man for endurance and constancy to prove whether he was good enough to get to California."[1]

The animals and plants that survive here are finely adapted to do so. The jackrabbit's paddle ears are lined with shallow blood vessels, which allow the air to cool its blood. Kangaroo rats seal their burrows to capture the precious moisture released when they breathe. Owls and vultures obtain water through the blood of their prey. The desert tortoise, which often digs its burrows under the shade and camouflage of creosote bushes, survives the harshest seasons of the Mojave by estivating: it gorges on cacti, grasses, and wildflowers during spring, then disappears into the cool darkness of its underground home and waits out the heat of summer.

Native Americans have lived in areas of the desert for at least 10,000 years, but humans have traditionally been sparse on the land. Until recently, our need for water limited human habitation to areas where it pooled and ran. The Mojave Indians congregated mostly along the spine of the Colorado River, a fact reflected in their traditional name, Pipa Aha *Macav*, which means "the people by the river." The nomadic *Chemehuevi* people, whose traditional lands include the Ivanpah Valley, are known as "those that play with fish." Human impacts were minimal until the arrival of miners and ranchers in the mid- to late-1800s. The Clark Mountains attracted swarms of grubstakers seeking silver, borax, copper, lead, tungsten, and fluorite. In the 1880s, the mining town of Ivanpah popped up near where the Ivanpah solar complex stands today. The town did a brisk trade: saloons, a butcher shop, hay yards, hotels, and a weekly newspaper. Around 1900, the minerals ran out and so did the people. The town was abandoned and the desert reclaimed the space.

Just as the seemingly empty and forbidding Mojave actually thrives with life, a desert that can appear bereft of industry in truth supports—and sometimes suffers—quite a lot of it. Though the town of Ivanpah never returned, the mining industry still survives here. Just over the shoulder of Clark Mountain sits the open pit Colosseum Mine, which operated from the early-1980s until 1993. A few kilometers south of Ivanpah is one of America's largest rare earth element mines, which produces the metals used in smartphones, high-efficiency light bulbs, and photovoltaic (PV) cells. Mining is no longer the major industry here, however. Today the area's economic engine is power production.

Look across the landscape. Just over the border in Primm is the Bighorn Generating Station, a 598-megawatt natural gas power plant completed in 2004. Next to it is the Silver State North Project, a 50-megawatt photovoltaic solar farm. When it opened in 2012, Silver State North became the first power-producing solar project on federal land. It's expected to be followed in the next few years by Silver State South, a 250-megawatt sister project, and by the 300-megawatt Stateline Solar Farm Project, a PV farm tucked between I-15 and the Ivanpah heliostats. The Ivanpah Valley is on track to become one of the most concentrated centers of power production in the American West.

RENEWABLE POWER IN THE DESERT

What does this activity mean to the desert landscape itself? It's complicated.

Let's start with the big picture: climate change. Prior to the Industrial Revolution, the Earth's atmosphere contained about

275 parts per million (ppm) of carbon dioxide. After centuries of burning coal and other fossil fuels, that figure rose to 316 ppm in 1959, the first year reliable carbon records were kept at the Mauna Loa observatory in Hawaii. We hit 350 ppm around 1990. In 2014, we're at 397 ppm and rising at a rate of two ppm every year. Carbon dioxide, methane, and other greenhouse gases are raising the Earth's global mean temperature, melting the polar ice caps, raising sea levels, acidifying the oceans, and increasing the intensity of droughts, wildfires, and coastal storms.

Humans are already being affected. Storms of greater frequency and violence, such as Katrina and Sandy, pummel coastal cities like New Orleans and New York. In the heartland, killer heat waves strike more often, last longer, and are expected to increase fivefold over the next forty years. Rising temperatures are allowing mosquitoes to expand their range, spreading malaria and dengue fever to previously untouched regions. Rising seas are flooding coastal towns in Alaska, forcing entire villages to relocate kilometers inland. Low-lying island countries like the Maldives have no inland to which they can flee. Maldivian leaders are now looking at buying property in Sri Lanka, India, and Australia, with an eye toward the day when rising seas force them to relocate the entire nation.

Other species are faring far worse. Climate change has been a catastrophe for polar bears who find their hunting grounds literally melting into the sea. The bears are climate change's most famous victims, but they're hardly the only species struggling. According to the World Wildlife Fund, over the past forty years the sizes of 10,000 representative populations of mammals, birds, reptiles, and fish have declined by 50%. Four decades, half the animals gone. Habitat loss, overhunting, and climate change were the causes. Birds are losing critical nesting ground all over the world. Higher temperatures, drier years, and extended drought wither the vegetation in Colorado's Gunnison Basin, which results in more nest failures among the endangered sage grouse. Rising seas and increasing storms threaten to wipe out the piping plover's coastal nesting and foraging habitat. These are but a few examples. Lists of species imperiled by climate change typically run on for dozens of pages.

The problem is so immense. How do we respond? We press for change and we do what we can, today. As Jamey and I were talking over our Mojave itinerary, hundreds of thousands of concerned citizens gathered in New York City for the world's largest demonstration for action on climate change. No one of us alone can reverse the entire planet's warming. But each of us contributes to its cause. NASA climate scientist James Hansen, who has been at the forefront of global warming research for decades, once summarized the challenge. "If humanity wishes to preserve a planet similar to that on which civilization developed and to which life on Earth is adapted," he wrote, "paleoclimate evidence and ongoing climate change suggest that CO2 will need to be reduced from its current [level] to at most 350 ppm."[2]

We can get there by cutting back our carbon burn. In the United States, we produce most of our energy—82%—by burning oil, coal, and natural gas. With every megawatt produced from those sources, more CO2 escapes into the atmosphere. Some forms (natural gas) are cleaner than others (coal), but the only sources that move us closer to James Hansen's goal are solar, wind, geothermal, hydroelectric, and nuclear power. Hydro's expansion options are limited, and the methane produced by new reservoirs undercuts their carbon-neutral aspect. Nuclear power has yet to solve its waste and safety issues, which makes it extremely difficult to finance and build new plants. Only solar, wind, and geothermal have the potential to take big chunks out of our carbon budget.

No energy source is perfect, though. Ramping up renewables requires real estate. Wind power only works in places with a consistent blow. Solar power needs acreage; you can't stack mirrors or photovoltaic panels one on top of another. Some of that space exists on rooftops. The expansion of distributed solar has gotten a boost from the plummeting price of solar PV modules, which has fallen by more than 80% since 2008. But rooftop solar has limits. If every house and commercial building in America harvested energy, they'd be able to meet only 60% of the nation's electrical demand. We need more conservation, rooftop solar, better efficiencies, and utility-scale wind and solar.

On the day Ivanpah opened, solar power accounted for only 0.4% of America's electricity budget. "There is an enormous gap between what needs to get done and what is actually happening on the ground," former BrightSource CEO John Woolard said during the plant's construction. "I don't think people really have digested how far behind we are from a policy perspective and how bad the consequences are. On a global basis we have got to put one gigawatt of zero carbon power online every single day between now and 2040 just to stabilize CO2 emissions. Given the size of our carbon footprint relative to that of the rest of the world, the US would have to add one gigawatt of zero carbon power each week."

That means land use. Ivanpah's heliostats range over fourteen square kilometers (3,500 acres) of publicly owned, federally managed desert landscape. That's four times the size of New York City's Central Park. The Silver State North PV farm covers two-and-a-half square kilometers. Stateline will shade another seven square kilometers.

There's no way of getting around it. Those are significant chunks of prime Mojave habitat. And therein lies the dilemma for environmentalists.

MICROS, MACROS, AND THE BATTLE JOINED

Over the past five years, increasing concern over climate change has given rise to a conservation schism between micro-enviros and macro-enviros. It's playing out in places like the Ivanpah Valley.

The micros know their own backyard on a species-by-species level. They are the riverkeepers and watershed watchers. For generations, these champions of the natural world pushed back against industrial pollution, unnecessary development, and roughshod trammeling. They saved countless species from extinction. They created national parks and our national wilderness system. They kept dams out of the Grand Canyon.

The macros sympathize with the micros, but they see a planet on fire. In their view, dousing the flame—i.e., cutting the carbon emissions that cause global warming—must be the first order of business. If you can't contain climate change, all those tens of thousands of micro conservation projects will be undone.

Ultimately, micros and macros are on the same side. They just believe those on the other side are undermining the cause they're fighting for.

Ivanpah has been their field of battle. Local environmental groups raised the alarm about losing 14 square kilometers of high-quality tortoise habitat to Ivanpah's footprint. The desert tortoise, *Gopherus agassizii*, is a long-lived and emblematic Mojave Desert species. It's been listed as "threatened" under the federal Endangered Species Act since 1980. In some areas, the desert tortoise population has decreased by as much as 90% in the past thirty years.[3] And the Ivanpah Valley, by all accounts, is excellent desert tortoise habitat.

That forced a number of environmental advocates, who usually champion solar power, to take a hard look at the Ivanpah project. Solar power "should go on rooftops or in appropriate places, not the pristine desert," said April Sall, director of the Wildlands Conservancy. "We need to tackle warming, but not forget there are other things at stake."[4] Local chapters of the Sierra Club found themselves divided on the issue. Some favored Ivanpah for its carbon-free energy; others thought the wildlife costs were too high. After BrightSource, Bechtel, and NRG agreed to a number of tortoise-mitigation measures, the national Sierra Club gave the project its blessing. "We need to jump-start renewables to combat climate change," said Sierra Club energy specialist Barbara Boyle, "and large-scale solar has to play a big role in that."[5]

Ultimately, though, it shouldn't be an either/or issue. As Ivanpah has proceeded, the project has become a critical test case for the proposition that large-scale renewable power plants can adapt to their surroundings and push back against global warming without trampling the local biota underfoot.

SOLAR FLUX AND RELATIVE RISK

At midday, Jamey and I drive into the heliostat field with NRG Operations Manager Len Cigainero. We stop at the boundary between the inner and outer ring of mirrors that bounce sunlight onto the boiler of Tower 2. "The inner ring is cleared and graded," Cigainero explains. "Beyond that it's left in as natural a state as possible." Jamey and I wander amid the concentric circles. Each heliostat contains two garage-door-size mirrors. "There's nothing that special about them," Cigainero tells me. "They're mirrors just like you'd have in your bathroom." Except much, much bigger.

As the day's heat reaches its peak, Len Cigainero leads Jamey and me 115 meters (376 feet) up Tower 2. Above us, the 570°C (1050°F) heat generated by the focused solar energy of 60,000 heliostats is creating superheated steam that cranks a power-producing turbine.

It's an awesome sight, standing at the rail, looking out at the mirror field—120,000 brilliant white cards, all pointed in our direction. I imagine it's something like Jimi Hendrix saw at Woodstock. It's an interesting vantage point to consider one of Ivanpah's environmental flashpoints: avian mortality. Wildlife advocates raised early concerns about the effect of Ivanpah's solar flux field on passing birds. Solar flux is a measure of the light energy in a given area. Ivanpah's solar flux field encompasses the airspace between the mirrors and the tower boilers. Ivanpah's heliostats don't create super-heated air. Air absorbs very little light energy. Any object placed in the solar flux field, though, will absorb light energy and convert it to thermal energy. Therein lies the risk to birds. If they fly through the flux field, close to the towers, they can singe their feathers and even catch fire.

Through the first six months of Ivanpah's operation, on-site biologists recorded 321 bird deaths. Of those, 133 were related to solar flux. That extrapolates to roughly 640 birds per year. That number is higher than anybody wants, and the companies operating Ivanpah are working to lower it. Biologists, using bird dogs, currently search the tower and heliostat areas daily to find and record avian carcasses, in order to get a better understanding of the problem. Engineers like Len Cigainero are trying new solutions like switching to LED bulbs on the towers at night, which might attract fewer insects—and fewer birds who feed on those bugs.

Ultimately, Ivanpah's bird issue comes down to a question of relative harm. The number of birds lost to solar flux pales in comparison to those killed in the United States by other anthropogenic causes. Each year, hundreds of millions die from window collisions, power lines, automobiles and trucks, communication towers, pesticides, oil and chemical spills, not to mention the significant impact of domestic and feral cats. But that comparison only gets us so far. It's more useful to measure concentrated solar plants like Ivanpah against other forms of power generation in a watt-by-watt comparison. Benjamin Sovacool, a Vermont Law School professor and energy policy analyst, has done just that. By looking at a wide range of data—from bird collisions with nuclear cooling towers, to wind turbine mortality, to the effects of mercury poisoning and acid rain—Sovacool came up with a set of figures that compares fossil fuel generation beside nuclear and wind power.

The estimates were astonishing. Fossil fuel power plants (coal, oil, natural gas) were responsible for 9.4 bird deaths per gigawatt hour (GWh) of power produced. Nuclear facilities were responsible for 0.6 avian fatalities per GWh. Wind turbines, which have a reputation for causing bird mortality, turned out to be significantly safer than fossil fuel power generation. Sovacool estimated that the turbine blades and towers were responsible for 0.3 avian mortalities per GWh.[6]

Sovacool didn't include concentrated solar power in his calculations. The technology was too new and the data simply didn't exist. But if we do some preliminary calculations based on an early, small sample size, Ivanpah's avian mortality lands somewhere in the wind turbine and nuclear power range. Ivanpah is expected to produce somewhere in the neighborhood of 1,000 gigawatt hours of power in a year. If all bird deaths are counted, that means the plant would be responsible for 0.6 avian fatalities per GWh; if only solar flux losses are counted, the figure comes down to 0.2.

This is a classic example of what I call the fallacy of visible harm. We see a bird with singed wings and are moved, rightly, to call for more protection for these imperiled creatures. But what we don't see are the millions of birds killed by the indirect forces—habitat loss, acid rain, mercury poisoning, and climate change—perpetuated by our continued addiction to fossil fuels. The comparison isn't even close; it's a full order of magnitude. Coal-fired and gas-fired power plants kill more than fifteen times as many birds per GWh as wind and solar facilities combined. The difference is, they're dying hundreds of kilometers from the source of their death. Birds can't make that connection. They don't possess the cognitive power. But we do. And so we take a hard look at the tradeoffs involved in the act of power generation, weigh the benefits and losses, and move ahead with the technology that promises the best outcome for ourselves and the environment around us.

HEAD START FOR THE DESERT TORTOISE

As the sun makes its first move toward the western horizon, Jamey and I drive over to Ivanpah's biological center, amodest collection of shipping-container offices and fenced tortoise habitats. This is Ivanpah's desert tortoise biological center, a place that's become known as the Desert Tortoise Head Start.

At Ivanpah, the desert tortoise acts as an umbrella species. The protocols taken to safeguard the reptiles and their habitat benefit a multitude of other species in the ecological web. NRG's permit from the US Bureau of Land Management allows them just nine desert tortoise "takings" (deaths) over Ivanpah's planned 30-year lifespan. They've already had one. "A biologist ran over a tortoise when doing a tortoise check," Cigainero told me earlier that morning. "The tortoises look for shade, and this one found it under the wheel of his parked truck." Ever since then, everybody on-site does a vehicle perimeter check before starting up.

It's not just direct hazards that Ivanpah workers have to watch out for. There are indirect dangers, too. "We're very careful about trash," Cigainero told me. "We work hard at making employees understand the importance of keeping the area trash-free in order to not attract ravens." Desert tortoises have a coterie of predators: ravens, kit foxes, coyotes, red-tailed hawks, golden eagles, badgers, and burrowing owls. A spilled Coke or a misplaced Carl's Jr. bag might be enough to draw these predators—especially ravens—to the site. And then their sharp eyes might spot a tasty tortoise.

At the biological station, Jamey and I meet up with Max Havelka, a biologist who oversees the juvenile tortoise pens. The heat of the day has come up, and Havelka's decked in full desert workwear: a wide-brimmed straw hat, extra-dark sunglasses, and a slathering of sunscreen. He tells me about the tortoise relocation operation that's been going on for four years now.

"This turned out to be better tortoise habitat than anyone imagined," he says. In the fall of 2010, before Bechtel broke ground on construction, a team of biologists scoured the Ivanpah site. Fall is typically an active time for tortoises who emerge from their long summer burrow to graze in the cooler autumn temperatures. The biologists gathered 173 adult and juvenile tortoises and relocated them to temporary holding pens in a one-and-three-quarters square kilometer (433 acre) preserve set aside for rare plants and wildlife. "We started with sixteen tortoise pens, and ended up with more than 100," Havelka tells me.

Tortoises have a slow and precarious reproductive cycle. They can take up to twenty years to reach sexual maturity, and females lay eggs only when environmental conditions are optimal. Most hatchlings don't survive. Researchers estimate that up to 98% of juvenile tortoises are killed by predators in their first years of life. That makes what happened after the tortoise-gather all the more curious and remarkable. Female tortoises in Ivanpah's temporary holding pens began laying eggs left and right. Maybe it was coincidental. Maybe it was a response to stress. Maybe the females looked around at the plentiful forage, water, and predator protection and thought...conditions optimal! Havelka and other biologists don't know for sure. What they do know is that by the spring of 2011 they had 53 new juveniles on their hands.

After fitting the adult tortoises with tiny transponders, Havelka and his colleagues released them back into the Ivanpah Valley, outside the heliostat fields. The transponders allow NRG's staff biologists to locate the reptiles and check on their health twice a year. To release the juveniles, though, would be to lose 98% of the next generation of a federally threatened species. So biologists like Havelka continue to nurture them behind protective fencing in what became known as the Head Start area, named after the US government program that provides early childhood education and healthcare to children in low-income families.

"We'll keep them here until their carapace reaches twelve centimeters in length," Havelka explains. That's about as long as a Pepsi can is tall. "At that point they're able to fend for themselves."

As we stroll through the Head Start area, it's tough to spot any tortoises. And yet we're surrounded by dozens of them. "There's one," Havelka says. A four-inch juvenile crawls glacially under the shade of a creosote bush. Desert tortoises live up to 95% of their lives underground, and when they do emerge, they exhibit none of the darting movements that alert predators to their presence. Rule of survival: you can't eat what you can't see.

Like a lot of conservationists, Havelka is aware of the tough tradeoffs involved in an industrial-scale renewable project like Ivanpah. He sees the gains and losses every day. The Mojave, he says, "...is amazing. It's like a desert version of an old-growth forest." It's an apt description. The Mojave's creosote bushes can thrive for centuries. They're drought-hardy and so oily that herbivores don't touch them. "King Clone," a Mojave Desert creosote bush ring, is believed to be one of the oldest living organisms on Earth. University of California, Riverside, botanist Frank Vasek, who discovered the bush in the late 1970s, has estimated the plant's age at around 11,700 years.[7]

Desert tortoises don't live quite that long, although in the wild they can survive for fifty years or more. Their survival into the next century, however, may depend on whether we can ramp up our renewable energy output—because they, too, are imperiled by climate change. Female tortoises lay fewer eggs during drought years, and soil temperatures affect the sex of embryos. Temperatures above 31.5°C (88.7°F) favor the development of females, so an increasing number of heat waves could leave the population here with a reproductive ratio problem. In other words, doing nothing about climate change is as risky to the long-term health of the desert tortoise as are the disturbances imposed by projects like Ivanpah Solar.

FADE TO BLACK

Late in the afternoon, Jamey and I climb into a Robinson R-44 and rise thousands of feet above the desert floor. As the horizon pulls the sun closer, the helicopter offers us yet another perspective on the Mojave. From 2,000 meters high we can see over and beyond Clark Mountain and the Castle Range, the two mountain bands that define and drain into the Ivanpah Valley. The light's low angle raises the contrast on the land. A multitude of dry creeks, washes, deer paths, Jeep trails, rail lines, and dirt roads crosshatch and serpentine over the terrain.

At 5:11, all three Ivanpah power blocks glow an eerie white. They're lit up like tall candles on a dining room table. Tiny movements ripple through the mirrors as the computer controlling the heliostats milks every last watt from the sinking sun.

Twenty minutes later the shadow of Clark Mountain reaches out across the valley floor, nearly touching the outer ring of Unit 3's heliostats. The darkness moves at a hiker's pace, slow but steady. All three power blocks blaze until finally, at 5:56, Unit 1 and Unit 3 begin to fade.

The end of the solar day arrives quickly. Within two minutes, the power block on Unit 3 is dark. Unit 2 still shines, but Unit 1 is fading fast. One minute later, Unit 1 is dark. By 6:03, all three tower boilers are black. Ivanpah is off the grid.

Back in the control room, NRG's engineering team closes out the day. One-by-one the heliostats move into sleep mode, standing vertically, reflecting darkness.

Meanwhile, in the desert, the nocturnal creatures start to emerge. As the intense heat of the day dissipates, they peek out of burrows, foxholes, and caves. Bats flutter into the evening sky. Tortoises crawl out of their holes to forage. The Mojave Desert stirs back to life.

As we take one last swoop over the darkening valley, it strikes me that the Mojave has found, in the desert tortoise, its perfectly emblematic species: one that captures all the slow vigor, fragility, reticence, deception, indomitability, and strange beauty of the desert. Like the desert itself, its wonders and charms aren't apparent upon first glance. It takes some time to learn, to understand, and to appreciate. The same might be said of the Ivanpah project. It's compelling, strange, and not easily comprehended. But it represents one of our best shots at getting right with the tortoise, the Mojave, and the planet. It's a step in the right direction.

NOTES

1. John Steinbeck, *Travels with Charley*. (New York: Bantam Books, 1963), 209. First published 1962 by Viking Press.
2. James Hansen, et al, "Target Atmospheric CO2: Where should humanity aim?" Open *Atmospheric Science Journal* 2 (2008): 217-31.
3. "Fact Sheet: Desert Tortoise," Defenders of Wildlife website, 2015.
4. Ken Wells, "Where Tortoises and Solar Power Don't Mix," *Bloomberg Businessweek*, October 10, 2012.
5. Ibid.
6. Benjamin K. Sovacool, "The Avian and Wildlife Costs of Fossil Fuels and Nuclear Power," *Journal of Environmental Sciences* 9, no. 4 (December 2012): 255-78.
7. Frank C. Vasek, "Creosote Bush: Long-Lived Clones in the Mojave Desert," *American Journal of Botany* 67, no. 2 (February 1980): 246-55.

CHANGING PERSPECTIVES

Jamey Stillings

In art, as in life, perspective is an essential ingredient of understanding. And if we think about it, understanding is a journey, not a point of arrival; as we add time, experience, and knowledge, our understanding evolves.

My first flight over the future site of Ivanpah Solar initiated such a process. From 2010 to 2014, I photographed this fourteen-square-kilometer section of the Mojave Desert as it was transformed into the world's largest concentrated solar power plant. Nineteen flights and several ground-based visits later, I see Ivanpah as symbolic of the promise and challenge we face in building a sustainable civilization, both for ourselves and future generations.

There were many potential stories to be told during Ivanpah's construction. No tower-style concentrated solar thermal plant of this scale had yet been built—a planned capacity of 392 megawatts. Over two thousand "green" construction jobs would be created as the country worked its way out of the Great Recession. And the decision to translocate desert tortoises off the site to other habitat was emblematic of the controversy surrounding a site on public land, adjacent to Interstate 15 and existing transmission lines, but, otherwise, relatively undisturbed. To capture these stories, I would need safe, but unfettered, entry to the construction site. Though requested and discussed, such access was not forthcoming.

Sometimes, limitations help me recognize a greater opportunity. I realized the airspace over the Ivanpah project was public, a space where I could observe and photograph with few restrictions. I decided to document Ivanpah's evolution from above. And thus began my four-year aerial survey.

Millions of us peek through the small windows of commercial airplanes at the passing urban, rural, and natural landscapes, but few have the opportunity to spend hours and days looking intently at the Earth below, visually interpreting what one observes through the viewfinder of a camera. Each of my flights over Ivanpah was in a small helicopter, the pilot and I a symbiotic team, weighing the visual goals of broad views and abstract details against the transitory nature of light and weather, all while keeping safety a priority.

I am drawn to first and last sunlight, as this oblique light best reveals the textures, changes, history, and secrets of the desert. This meant careful planning was essential. The North Las Vegas Airport, from which we flew, is a thirty-to-forty-minute flight from Ivanpah. To arrive before dawn, with enough time to scout the site's progress and be ready to catch first sunlight, required discipline and adherence to a strict schedule. Once the light was up, my sense of urgency mixed with the desire to intuitively interpret the landscape beneath me. Time was short. As the sun rose into the sky, shadows shortened, and the scene quickly became ordinary.

Late afternoon photography required a different set of calculations. We needed sufficient fuel to photograph over the site through prime light, while keeping enough in reserve to later fly safely north. The weight of the pilot, photographer, equipment, and fuel impacted our time aloft, as did the hot air temperatures of summer months. If no clouds blocked the waning sun, my photography started slowly, then worked to a more and more frenetic pace as the sun descended toward the western mountains. Tight shots gave way to bigger views, as the evening drama of the Mojave landscape was once again revealed.

Each new trip built upon previous visits, fresh imagery layering upon and interacting with earlier work. Geometric forms of boundary fencing, service roads, and reshaped earth gradually intersected, transformed, or subsumed the organic forms of desert vegetation and erosion gullies descending through alluvial slopes to the dry lake basin. Steadily, the structures of a solar power plant emerged. Three 140-meter towers grew, centers for their respective solar fields, while thousands of heliostats (mirrors) were installed around each.

As Ivanpah took form within the desert landscape, my photo-essay grew in depth and amplitude. So, too, did my knowledge of the plant's concentrated solar thermal power technology: its strengths, potential, and limitations; environmental concerns about its siting and operation; and the politics for and against utility-scale renewable energy development. My perspective has evolved, as has my understanding.

While black and white represent the tonal end points of imagery in this book, shades of gray bring structure, detail, and nuance to each photograph. And while our rash obsession in contemporary culture is to embrace extreme positions, real progress lies in understanding the importance and great complexity found between these poles.

Over thousands of years, *Homo sapiens* have evolved to dominate, though not control, the Earth's ecosystem. We utilize its diverse and precious resources for both constructive and destructive ends. It is easy, and perhaps reflexive, to respond to such changes in absolutes, but a more reasoned approach may be to realize such transformations elicit differing and, often, dissonant responses. We may be intrigued, inspired, indeed seduced, by changes made to the land as we establish an order, pattern, or structure that provides utility for ourselves and our culture. Yet, we may also be challenged by what these transformations entail.

Developing renewable energy capacity, whether on rooftops or as large utility-scale projects around the world, represents another important phase in this transformation. We cannot predict the future impact or results from such efforts. However, by observing and documenting these contemporary changes, I endeavor to create imagery relevant both to our present-day collective conversation, and to a future historical perspective of this era on Earth. *The Evolution of Ivanpah Solar* is but the first chapter of a larger, global project called *Changing Perspectives*, which will document renewable energy over the next several years. I look forward to continuing the conversation.

ACKNOWLEDGMENTS

Behind every dedicated photographer is a group of essential people who assist, collaborate, support, and facilitate a project. *The Evolution of Ivanpah Solar* exists today, as a body of work and a book, because of the tremendous generosity of many who gave of their time, energy, and experience. In the years since my first flight over Ivanpah, this community continues to grow and evolve. I am grateful for the great friendships, old and new, that enrich my life and work.

Danke sehr to Gerhard Steidl for responding to my work, the book maquette, and agreeing to create this book with me. I admire and appreciate Gerhard's dedication to the art of photography book publishing. A great book requires the dedication of many, so thanks, also, to the staff of Steidl Verlag for their shared commitment to excellence in each step of the process.

Thanks to David Chickey of Skolkin + Chickey for our collaboration in developing and realizing the concept and design of this book. Beyond David's design expertise, I value his wise insight and advice. Thanks, also, to Timothy Edeker for his help.

A special thank you to my late mother and father, Mary and Edwin Stillings, for their great gift of life, and for encouraging me to take on the world with a sense of curiosity, creativity, and adventure. And to my sisters, Chrystal Smith and Kathryn Stillings, who generously give me their love, advice, and support.

In the studio, Dianne Duenzl and Bill Stengel are an amazing, enthusiastic, and supportive team. Steve Zeifman of Rush Creek Editions works closely with me to create beautiful exhibition prints.

Finally, the biggest thanks goes to Esha Chiocchio, my wonderful wife, and to Zubin and Ciela, our amazing children. Their love, encouragement, and support bring me the greatest joy in life.

For Their Thoughtful and Valued Contributions to This Book

Anne Wilkes Tucker, Robert Redford, and Bruce Barcott

For Their Enthusiastic Belief in and Support of the Work

The New York Times Magazine
Kathy Ryan

photo-eye Gallery
Rixon Reed, Anne Kelly, and Melanie McWhorter

Etherton Gallery
Terry Etherton, Hannah Glasston, Dawne Osborne, and Daphne Srinivasan

The United States Library of Congress
Helena Zinkham and Verna Curtis

photokunst
Barbara Cox and Anne Sheridan

For Their Skillful Helicopter Piloting and Assistance

Matt Binner, Mike Garavaglia, Aaron Hamm, Leslie Hortman, and Jacquelin Mass

For Facilitating Communication about Ivanpah Solar

BrightSource Energy, Inc.
H. David Ramm, Joseph Desmond, Jennifer Z. Rigney, Hagai Huss, Israel Kroizer, John Woolard, Keely Wachs, Kristin Hunter, Jared Blanton, and Michael Bobinecz

For Their Encouragement, Insights, and Support

Mary Anne Redding, Mary Virginia Swanson, Ann Alexander and Richard Khanlian, Rhea Anna, Elizabeth Avedon, Blue Earth, Susan Burnstine, Julian Cox, Sam Deaner, William Ewing, Peter Fahrni, Debbie Fleischaker, Benjamin Füglister, Patricia Galagan and Philip Metcalf, Juan Alberto Gaviria, Hamidah Glasgow, Adam Goff, Elda Harrington, Bridget Harris, Brooks Jensen, Hideko Kataoka, Natalie Matutschovsky, Dee Ann McIntyre, Michelle Molley, Laura Moya, New Mexico Council on Photography, Tim Nisly, Claire O'Neill, Stephanie Pugash, Mitch Samuelian, Wilson Scanlan, Aline Smithson, Luise Stauss, Juan Travnik, and Katherine Ware

First edition published in 2015

Book Design: David Chickey
Separations: Steidl's digital darkroom
Production and printing: Steidl, Göttingen

Cover photograph: #9499, 21 March 2013

To see additional work by Jamey Stillings, please visit:
www.jameystillingsprojects.com.

Steidl
Düstere Str. 4 / 37073 Göttingen, Germany
Phone +49-551-49 60 60 / Fax +49 551 49 60 649
mail@steidl.de
steidl.de

ISBN 978-3-86930-913-2
Printed in Germany by Steidl

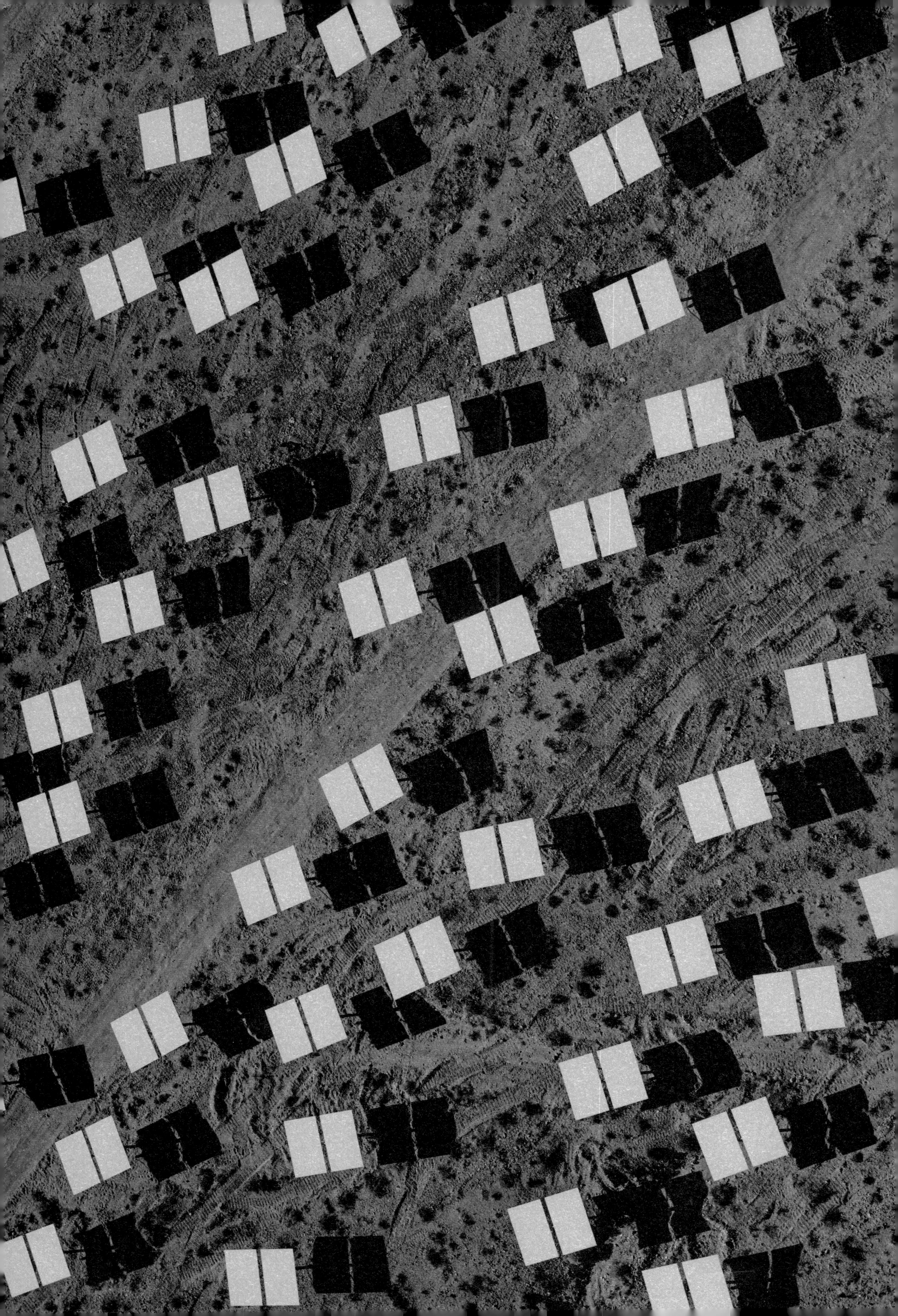

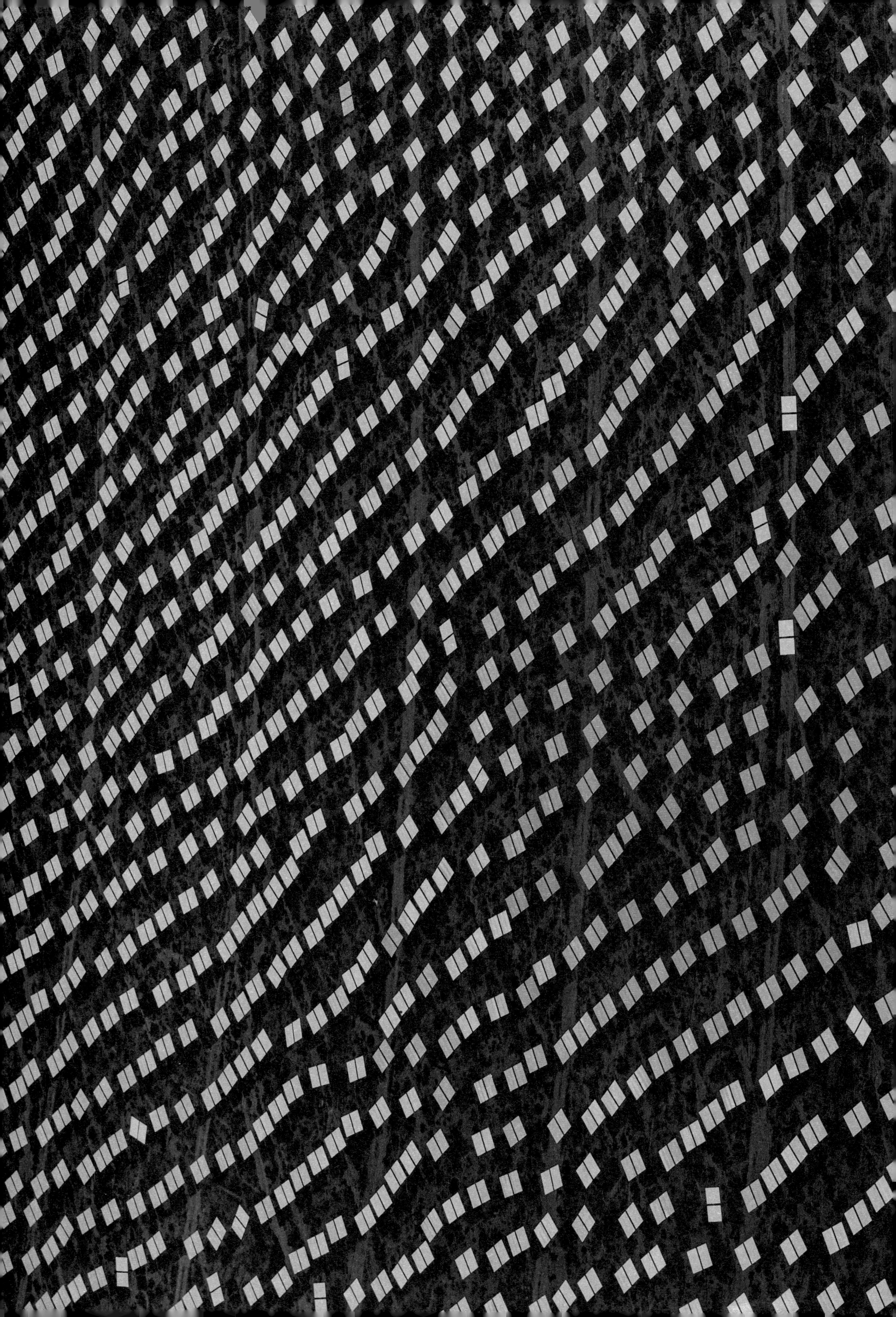